"WHAT AM I GOING TO DO ABOUT MY FEAR?"

"My worst fear is being enclosed. The door on a plane shutting is by far the strongest panic cue for me. Also, the longer the flight the more uptight I am."

—Sherry, Age 36

"My fear is getting on any plane. I shudder at the thought. It isn't even easy for me to go to airports unless I am 100% sure I won't have to get on the plane—even for a moment."

—Tony, Age 42

"I have never liked to fly. Turbulence and the thought of getting airsick are my fears. If the flight is even a little bumpy—it's a sure panic attack for me. I just stare at the FASTEN SEAT BELT sign, waiting for it to light up."

—Beth, Age 27

SHERRY, TONY, AND BETH ALL CONQUERED THEIR FEARS. LIKE THEM YOU CAN DISCOVER THE SIMPLE FOUR-STEP FORMULA THAT WILL HELP YOU DEVELOP YOUR OWN PERSONAL RECOVERY PLAN. IT'S EASY, IT WORKS, AND IT'S ALL IN—

LEARNING TO FLY WITHOUT FEAR

D1452496

"Informative and accurate, *Learning to Fly Without Fear* gives an excellent look into traveling by air. The author does an excellent job explaining how to overcome a fear of flying."

Daniel Z. Henkin
Vice President
AIR TRANSPORT ASSOCIATION
OF AMERICA

Most Berkley Books are available at special quantity discounts for bulk purchases for sales promotions, premiums, fund raising, or educational use. Special books or book excerpts can also be created to fit specific needs.

For details, write or telephone Special Markets, The Berkley Publishing Group, 200 Madison Avenue, New York, New York 10016; (212) 951-8800.

LEARNING TO FLY WITHOUT FEAR

Ken Hutchins

BERKLEY BOOKS, NEW YORK

LEARNING TO FLY WITHOUT FEAR

A Berkley Book / published by arrangement with
the author

PRINTING HISTORY
Berkley trade paperback edition / April 1990

All rights reserved.
Copyright © 1990 by Ken Hutchins.
Book design by Sheree Goodman.
This book may not be reproduced in whole or in part, by
mimeograph or any other means, without permission.
For information address: The Berkley Publishing Group,
200 Madison Avenue, New York, New York 10016.

ISBN: 0-425-12057-0

A BERKLEY BOOK® TM 757,375
Berkley Books are published by The Berkley Publishing Group,
200 Madison Avenue, New York, New York 10016.
The name "BERKLEY" and the "B" logo
are trademarks belonging to Berkley Publishing Corporation.

PRINTED IN THE UNITED STATES OF AMERICA

10 9 8 7 6 5 4 3 2 1

CONTENTS

PREFACE

There are estimated to be over twenty-five million people who are afraid to fly.

During my years as manager of training for a major airline it was frustrating to see the many people who suffered this fear and hated the thought of getting aboard an airplane. As a pilot I discussed the problem with many flight crews and learned that there are uncomfortable people on just about every commercial flight.

Some years ago I changed professions. I am now a licensed psychotherapist and have taught at various colleges and universities. During the many classes and workshops I have conducted I learned that there is much that can be done to help the person who is afraid to fly.

Learning to Fly Without Fear will provide you with practical advice and will explain how to deal effectively with your fear of flying. You will learn about airplanes, flying, and how to recognize and control fear.

Traveling by air is the fastest, most efficient, safest, and often the most economical and comfortable means of transportation available.

"According to a Massachusetts Institute of Technology study reported in *Scientific American*, the odds of being injured when traveling in an airplane are 1 in 2,599,000. You would have to take two flights a day for 3,560 years to use up all your chances."

Flying magazine

LEARNING TO FLY WITHOUT FEAR

1
FLYING AND SAFETY

Before we learn how to handle fears of flying, we need to understand a little about aviation. There is no need to trace events all the way back to the Wright brothers and their first flight. Our story can begin with the first airline service in the United States.

The first scheduled airline trip in the United States was between Boston and New York City in 1927 by a firm called Colonial Air Transport. These first scheduled flights were to deliver the U.S. mail. The planes were small, noisy, and generally unreliable.

The airline industry as we know it today began as a number of small independent airplane companies. Gradually more and more people began to accept the idea that aviation might service more than stuntmen and daredevils. Still, flying was only for the fearless traveler. Pilots flew by looking at the ground to find out where they were, and schedules were more guesses and hopes than reality. But things would quickly change.

The Ford Motor Company started making

airplanes and in 1933 introduced a plane called the Curtiss Condor. The Condor was the first plane designed to carry passengers. But the Condor did not fly smoothly. It was always bouncing up and down. In order to convince people to fly, some creative airline employees hired pretty girls with nurse's training to help the passengers who got motion sickness from all the bouncing up and down. These nurse-stewardesses also served coffee, tea, and meals to passengers.

Soon more and more airline companies began to pop up, aircraft grew larger and schedules became more reliable. People began to think of airplanes as a way to travel efficiently and safely. The government even joined in and began building airports.

Then came World War II. The needs of the military forced the aviation industry ahead. Bombers, fighters, and troop transports were built by the thousands and people became accustomed to flying as a regular means of transportation. After the war, there was a surplus of airplanes and trained pilots. Compared to the prewar days, flying was booming.

Today, in addition to the roughly thirty major carriers, there are over a hundred smaller commuter-type carriers operating in the U.S. Added to this are the air freight carriers, business airplanes, charter operations, sight-seeing companies, police aircraft, blimps, parachutists, military planes, crop dusters, private planes, fire-fighting planes, balloons, helicopters, and spaceships. Nowadays you can get a plane to go just about anywhere and do almost anything. Aviation is the seventh largest industry in the United States. Following agriculture, aircraft and aircraft parts are this country's second largest export.

> "In addition to moving nine out of every ten first-class letters and over five million tons of high-value freight, the U.S. airlines, with more than three hundred thousand employees, continue their role as the dominant public transportation mode, carrying 350 million passengers over 300 billion miles each year."
>
> Robert Aaronson
> President and Chief Executive Officer
> Air Transport Association

There are two types of commercial carriers—scheduled air carriers and charter carriers. The difference between scheduled air carriers and charters is that charters do not fly at regular times. Charters fly whenever there are enough people to fill the plane and wherever those people want to go. Charter prices are usually, but not always, lower than the fares charged by scheduled carriers. And, charter flights are just as safe as the scheduled airlines.

Private airplanes and corporate aircraft belong to the category known as general aviation. All airplanes that are not military or do not belong to a commercial carrier are general-aviation aircraft.

As you can see, aviation is very big business. Aviation is affected in one way or another by virtually every branch of our government. The Federal Aviation Administration (FAA) is the part of the United States Department of Transportation that takes care of air transportation.

To get the job done, the FAA must perform many duties. The FAA certifies all pilots, maintenance schools, repair stations, and aircraft. A special branch of the FAA conducts research and sponsors engineering and development programs to improve safety, air-traffic control and our environment.

The FAA constantly checks what it has certified. If an aircraft is found to be unsafe, the FAA issues what it calls airworthiness directives: the problem must be corrected or the airplane will be grounded. The FAA will not let unsafe airplanes fly. In the U.S., nothing can leave the ground unless the FAA deems it safe. By the way, foreign aircraft flying into the United States are subject to the same rigid standards required of domestic aircraft.

The FAA also plays a role in helping to further the export sales of American aircraft. This is no small matter, since 72 percent of all the world's commercial aircraft and 90 percent of the world's general-aviation aircraft are manufactured in the United States.

Government agencies can be confusing and frustrating to deal with because of their size and complexity. The important thing for you to remember is that thousands of people and millions of dollars are spent for one primary purpose—to make flying safe.

The Number One Concern Is Safety

Let us take a look at flying and see if we can clear up some of the myths.

First, flying *is* safe. You may not think it is; you may have feelings that it isn't—but it is, it's very safe. As a matter of fact, and I do mean fact, flying is the safest means of transportation available. Flying is safer than highways, safer than boats, safer than railroads, dogsleds, or walking. Aviation is the world's safest transportation system.

The airline transportation system is not only safe, it is comfortable. The American Medical Association even suggests that elderly people use air transportation as the least stressful way of traveling. Indeed, the average age of people who travel on tours is over fifty-five years old. It is not at all uncommon for businessmen to travel over one hundred thousand miles per year, year after year after year.

How can it be that many people think flying is unsafe when the facts show that it is safe? To a great extent, this is because flying has a long history of bad press.

Just think about the films and books about flying: *The High and the Mighty, Combat in the Air*. Or how about *The President's Plane Is Missing*? And don't forget the television programs—*And I Alone Survived* or *Murder on Flight 502*. Add to this the countless war stories of airplanes crashing into the sea or exploding in flight and the problem becomes even clearer.

5

What never makes the headlines, though, is the fact that a commercial flight departs safely every seventeen seconds each and every day.

Maybe we need to use a little sensationalism to point out how safe flying really is. Do you know that each year approximately five thousand more people are hit by trains than die aboard airplanes? More people drown in their own bathtubs than die flying. More people, in fact, die each year walking across the street than have been injured in airline accidents in the last ten years.

Traveling by scheduled airline is approximately twenty-five times safer than driving your automobile. "Sure," people will say, "there are more automobile accidents than there are airplane accidents. But in airplane accidents everybody dies." Wrong. Over the past twenty-five years, there have been survivors in more the 60 percent of all the accidents involving U.S. scheduled airlines. About 25 percent of aircraft accidents had no fatalities at all.

Yet people continue to insist that flying is unsafe. The truth is that an airplane is a safe place to be should there be a crash. Several years ago an airliner accidentally flipped over on its back traveling at 120 miles per hour. No one was even hurt. Now imagine sitting inside an automobile that flipped upside down while traveling 120 miles per hour.

The odds of being in an airline accident are approximately 4,500,000 to 1 in your favor. The facts prove flying is safe. And yet the myths continue.

Maybe part of the problem is the notoriety that comes when we hear of famous people who do not like to fly. And there is no shortage of famous people who would rather keep both feet on the ground—Irving Wallace, Stanley Kubrick, Tony Curtis, Liz Carpenter, Glenda Jackson, Maureen Stapleton, Jackie Gleason, Bob Newhart, John Madden, Spencer Tracy, and Judy Garland to name a few.

The Crew

Could our fears be about the people who fly the airplanes—those unknown people who are temporarily in charge of our life? Let's see who these people are and what it takes to become an airline captain.

Airline pilots fly between forty-five and fifty-five hours per month. To many people that really doesn't sound like very much work, but it is. No other profession requires a person to pass as many tests per year. An airline pilot's job is on the line every day. He must pass a minimum of six rigorous tests each and every year he flies. In addition to Class I physical examinations and flight proficiency checks, the FAA may, without notice, board any flight at any time to observe the captain and his crew. Failure on any part of any test could mean an immediate end to the pilot's flying career.

"I have been flying now for some thirty-five years. I have some eighteen thousand hours as a pilot and each year, without fail, I must pass a comprehensive physi-

7

cal ... I also must spend two days in our Denver training facility for proficiency training every other year. And, of course, there are also ongoing proficiency checks. Should I fail to measure up, I'm either re-trained and rechecked to proficiency or I'm grounded. Of course, this rule applies to all our pilots. It's tough and it's expensive—but in this business, it's all safety. If we can't operate safe, we can't operate."

Captain Bill Traub
Director, Flight Operations
United Airlines

As you can see, training is a continual part of an airline pilot's life. Pilots are some of the best-trained and most competent professionals in the world.

Listen to what one director of training has to say:

"Our pilot training far exceeds the FAA requirements. I personally think that to-day's flight crews are some of the—if not the—best-trained professionals in the world. Our youngest captains have at least seven years of training and some seven thousand plus hours' experience. A DC-10 pilot here at Continental will have twenty-five to thirty years' experience and some thirty thousand hours of total pilot-in-command time accumulated.

"I myself, like all the other pilots, must pass a physical and constantly receive checks and recurrent training. And, I have been flying now for twenty-six years. I

guess we believe we never can be perfect
. . . but we are awful darn close."

Captain Bob Lemon
Director, Flight Standards
and Training
Continental Airlines

Checks and Double Checks

An hour or more before a flight departs, the
flight crew arrives at the dispatch office to check
weather reports, route charts, the weight of the
airplane, the number of passengers, and the
amount of fuel necessary to complete their flight
safely. By the way, every airline is required by
law to carry enough fuel to reach its destination, fly around for forty-five minutes, and then
still be able to fly to a predetermined alternate
airport.

After making sure that the paperwork, the
weather, and the route of the flight are all okay,
the crew then proceeds to the airplane. Before
each and every departure, the airplane is physically inspected by the crew. Once on board,
the crew follows a very specific list called a
preflight checklist. Prior to departure, the
crew checks and double checks well over one
hundred separate items.

The flight crew of a modern jet usually consists of three professionals: the pilot, the copilot, and a flight engineer. The pilot and copilot
are both fully qualified to fly the plane. The
flight engineer, who is also a licensed commercial pilot, serves as a sort of technical director
and navigator.

The stewardesses and stewards on board are not there just to provide drinks and magazines. Stewardesses and stewards are also well-trained professionals and are quite capable of handling most emergencies. All cabin crew members receive first-aid training. If you have any physical problem while flying, the crew is trained and ready to help you.

"Our training at United Airlines is extensive. All cabin personnel are retrained in emergency and medical procedures each year. Of course we do our best to make each flight comfortable, but our primary purpose is safety."

Karen Mumm
Flight Attendant
United Airlines

While the flight crew is checking the routes and inspecting the airplane, while the engineer is checking to make sure all the cockpit equipment works correctly and the proper amount of fuel is on board, while the stewardesses and stewards are preparing the cabin, while all the crew are checking the literally thousands of safety devices on board the airplane, the ground crew is checking the passengers. Passengers are screened and no one is allowed on the airplane who is rowdy, intoxicated, or, in the opinion of the airline personnel, not suited for air travel. Passengers and luggage are also inspected to ensure no weapons are taken aboard.

The Airplane

Now, what about the airplane? Is it safe?

The design of today's commercial airliners provides backup systems for every essential part of the airplane. This means that if one system fails, there is an alternate system that can function equally as well as the first system. Duplication is the key to airline safety. All communication and navigational aids are duplicated. The human-error factor is brought to a bare minimum because the captain and the copilot each has his or her own separate instruments and controls.

Safety is built into all aircraft by the manufacturer. Twin-engine airliners are designed to fly safely on one engine. Four-engine airplanes will fly safely on two engines.

Pilots are constantly in radio contact with ground control. A typical commercial jet is equipped with more than half a million dollars' worth of electronic navigation equipment. Large jets like the 747 have three navigational systems similar to those that guided the Apollo spacecraft to the moon and back. Any one of these navigational systems can provide completely automatic guidance in any weather to any point on the earth.

Airplanes receive constant attention and maintenance by licensed mechanics. There is so much preventive maintenance, so much care, so much testing and replacing of parts, that there is literally no such thing as an old airplane.

If you were to maintain your car the way airlines maintain a plane, you would need three full-time mechanics to inspect your car every time you drove. You would have to replace each tire every 500 miles and tune the engine every 2,500 miles. You would have to completely disassemble your engine, change you brakes, take the transmission apart, and complete a general overall servicing every 10,000 miles. At 25,000 miles you would have to throw your "old" engine away and get another one.

To keep the average commercial aircraft flying, the maintenance alone costs over one million dollars per plane per year. For every hour an airplane is in flight, it receives the equivalent of five hours of maintenance.

How Airplanes Fly

Regardless of the size or type, all airplanes fly according to the same principles. Airplanes do not fly just because they go down the runway fast. In fact, many small planes can take off at speeds around fifty miles per hour. Now, your car doesn't fly at fifty miles per hour. But put some wings on your car and watch out.

Airplane wings are made with curved surfaces called airfoils. When air passes over the top of the curved wing, less-than-normal air pressure is produced. Nature always tries to equalize air pressure. The equalizing of air pressure produces what is called lift. Airplanes are literally *lifted* into the air.

To keep air moving constantly over the wings, at least one engine is required. Generally speaking, there are two types of engines: engines with propellers and jet engines. Both engines are equally safe. Propeller engines are a lot like the engine in your car, except that they are probably much better maintained. Jet engines are more efficient than propeller engines and are more common.

The principle of the jet engine is simple. Air is drawn into the front of the jet engine, where it is heated, compressed, and then forced out of the rear faster than it went in the front. The result is a forward movement, or thrust.

The people who design airplanes, aeronautical engineers, design planes so that even if all the engines quit at the same time (and remember, each engine is independent and has many backup systems), the plane could still fly and land.

A Final Word on Safety

So we can see that the airlines are safe. Years of accident-free operation have proven that today's aircraft are safe. The pilots and the crew are very well trained and competent. All airplanes have backup systems—and the maintenance is superb.

Federal regulations stipulate that "pilots in command have not only the right, but the obligation, to decline any flight operation which in their best judgment cannot be safely initiated and completed."

Next time you are on a flight and there is a delay, consider that the delay is probably to increase the safety of the flight. At worst, a delay is usually just an inconvenience. You should be glad that your captain has one paramount objective—and that is safety.

"Safety must and will remain the highest priority in the national air transportation systems."
Robert Aaronson
President and Chief Executive Officer
Air Transport Association

The airlines are businesses and, as businesses, try to make as much money as they can. In the long run, the only way for an airline to make money is to run a safe operation. In the airline business, safety equals profit.

2
PREFLIGHT PLANNING

We have learned that airplanes and flying are very safe. What we need to know now is how to plan our flights so that they are as comfortable and convenient as possible.

Airline Competition

As we have learned, an airline's prime concern is safety. Some people might disagree, arguing that an airline is a business and, as such, its prime concern is making a profit. No argument, I agree. But you cannot make money unless you operate successfully, right? In the airline industry, success equals safety.

In addition to operating safely, the airlines must compete with one another for your business. This competition breeds competitive services. Airlines try to outdo each other, and each creates a different image in order to convince you to buy your tickets from it.

If someone has a particularly good or bad experience on one flight, he will probably form a generalized bias for or against that entire airline. "Such and such an airline never leaves on time." "ABC Airline has the best food." "All the stewardesses on Zip-Zap Air are really unfriendly." So making your decisions based on what your neighbor tells you isn't very fair. You'll probably be better off making your own judgments based on your own experiences.

Each airline works hard to ensure that you do not get a bad impression of it. Airlines are continuously training their people to be friendly, courteous, and efficient. If you have a problem or special request, you will discover that most airlines are ready to help. And, if an airline makes a mistake or causes you some inconvenience, it will usually do its best to correct the problem. I'm not saying airlines are perfect—they aren't. Baggage is lost, flights are late, and reservations can disappear as if by magic. All things considered, though, airlines overall do a great job.

"Airlines strive to provide safe, efficient and economical transportation and, by and large, I think we do an excellent job. When a problem does occur we are very concerned to see that the problem is corrected and ensure all passengers are treated fairly. It is unfortunate that some people are quick to form a bad opinion about an airline based on one or two experiences. I think I can safely speak for most airlines when I ask that if you, as a passenger, are not satisfied with your flight and especially if you have some problem, please let us hear from you."

Frank Borman
Former President
Eastern Airlines

Fares and Reservations

Making airline reservations and getting the best price can be very confusing. Who flies to what cities and what do you do if you don't know? Well, there are a number of things you can do. First, you can call the airline you think flies where you're going. If you guess wrong, the airline you called will most likely give you the name of the proper airline to call. Unless you like to gamble, this really isn't the best way to go. Airline reservation telephone lines are often busy. Once you get through, if you guessed wrong, then you have to look up another number and then it's back to the telephone. If there are a number of different airlines going your way, then you might end up with three or four telephone calls to get one reservation.

A Sad Story

I wanted to fly from Seattle to Chicago on a Saturday. I thought TWA flew there. I called directory assistance to get TWA's telephone number. TWA didn't fly from Seattle to Chicago. If I wanted to go on TWA, I would have to travel via San Francisco. I asked what airline, if any, flew direct. I was told I could call Northwestern, Continental, and United. I thanked TWA and called directory assistance to get the reservation numbers for Northwestern, Continental, and United. I called United, and they told me their direct flight for next Saturday was full. I then called Northwestern, who said they could get me to Chicago on Saturday. I asked the fare and was booked on a Saturday morning departure, coach class.

Once aboard the flight, I discovered that direct does not always mean nonstop. I was in a small, crowded plane, the only non-smoker sitting in the smoking section. I had paid the wrong fare (I could have purchased an excursion fare ticket for $175). My flight would take nine hours rather than the nonstop time of five and a half hours.

Then, to top it all off, I discovered that Air Canada leaves from an airport near my house—less money and a nonstop flight.

And it can happen. If you travel a lot, you will eventually learn how to get the lowest fare, the best routing, and preferred services. These lessons are expensive, time-consuming, and very, very frustrating.

Here's an example of an "easy" trip to give you an idea of how complex planning a flight can become.

QUESTION: Who flies from Chicago to New Orleans and what is the lowest fare for a flight if I leave on a Friday before 10:00 A.M. and return a week later with a stop in Detroit, Michigan?

ANSWER: You could travel on five different airlines. If you purchase your ticket in advance you can save about thirty dollars, but you must return a day earlier than you had planned. If you fly at night, the fare is lower, but you must make three en route stops. Two airlines offer special discount fares, but neither will allow you to stop in Detroit on your way home. Depending on which airline, routing, class of service, and time of departure, there are thirty-eight possible different fares.

The easiest answer is to call a travel agent. Travel agents can make reservations and sell you tickets on any carrier, and the ticket will cost the same whether you buy it from a travel agent or directly from an airline.

The easiest way to locate a travel agent is probably in the Yellow Pages of a local telephone directory or through a reference from a friend. Ask around and find a travel agent you feel is professional and trustworthy. The quality and services vary from agent to agent, so shop around. Most reputable travel agents belong to the American Society of Travel Agents.

You must be specific about your travel requests. Unless you specifically ask, a travel agent might not book you on the most convenient and economical flight. A travel agent can tell you about advance seating, discount fares, which type of plane you will be flying on, and arrival and departure times. You can also ask about meals, movies, seating arrangements, and whether or not the plane has a smoking section. I think you will find most travel agents friendly and competent. If you have stopovers en route, remember to ask how long the stopovers will be. You wouldn't want to wait three hours at an airport halfway between where you left and where you are going. Nonstop flights are the fastest and are more likely to leave and arrive as scheduled. If you must change carriers to complete a trip, check connection times and make sure you have enough time to make your connection.

The airlines are required by law to quote you the lowest applicable fare. The catch is, you have to ask. If you miss a flight, hold on to your ticket. Most airline tickets are refundable for up to one year. You can also use one ticket in exchange for another.

Special or discount fares can be real money savers. There are a wide variety of special fares, and they are always changing. The travel section of your local newspaper should list promotional fares. Remember, shop around and ask questions.

Excursion flights are bargains if you are going to be gone a certain length of time, usually a week or a month or more. The idea behind excursion fares and advance-purchase fares is that you buy your ticket in advance and commit yourself to coming and going on certain preselected dates.

Most airlines also offer substantial discounts if you are traveling with your family or a group. And then there are packaged tours where the hotel and airfare are combined and sold together at a saving. Packaged tours may also include such items as meals, rental cars, and sight-seeing attractions. Again, ask the airline or travel agent.

Fares change rapidly. Discounts come and go. For example, a ticket from Los Angeles to Hawaii recently ranged from $69 to $450. My advice, find a good travel agent and ask a lot of questions.

Types of Planes

Each type of airplane has certain characteristics. Depending on what makes you comfortable, the choice of plane can make a big difference.

Normally, the smallest type of plane that you can buy a ticket for is a twin-engine commuter plane. These commuter-type planes usually carry six to twenty people, fly at around two hundred miles per hour, and travel between small cities. These planes are usually a little noisy and cramped. Fortunately, most commuter flights are only short hops, almost always less than an hour. Sometimes commuter flights are only ten to fifteen minutes long.

An uncrowded, short commuter flight might be a good first step, especially for people who have never flown. Pick a nice day and let the airline attendant know it's your first flight. If the length of the flight is of concern to you, ask the airline or travel agent how long the flight will take.

More than likely, though, you will be flying on a jet. Jets are by far the most common type of plane used by commercial carriers. A typical jet cruises at around six hundred miles per hour and carries about a hundred people. If you were flying from New York to Boston, or from San Francisco to Las Vegas, you would probably be flying on one of the medium-sized jets.

All of today's modern jet aircraft are comfortable and quiet. Because jets fly high above the earth, where the air is thin and cold, these planes are pressurized and heated. Having a pressurized cabin means that no matter how high the plane flies, the "altitude" inside the plane is kept just about the same as when you departed. As the cabin crew will explain each and every time you depart, oxygen masks are available in the event that the cabin loses pressure.

Commercial jets all have individual reading lights, air vents, tray tables, window shades, reclining seats, and at least one toilet.

Then there is the jumbo jet—for many fearful flyers, the answer to their prayers. There are different makes of jumbo jets. These planes are also called wide-bodies because of their incredible spaciousness. All of these remarkable airplanes are extremely quiet and very comfortable. The Boeing 747 even has an upstairs dining room, and the DC-10's kitchen is downstairs—and the stewards and stewardesses get there by elevator.

The single biggest advantage of the wide-body jet for the person who doesn't like to fly is that the sensation of flight is almost completely eliminated. The cabin is very large and is much more like the inside of a movie theater than a plane. The takeoffs and landings are smooth and quiet. Believe me, it's easy to forget you are even on a plane. On jumbo-jet flights, it's quite normal to get up and walk around, go to the stand-up bar, visit the lounge, or watch a movie.

If you've never been on a jumbo jet, you're in for a pleasant surprise.

"Wide-body jets offer a complete new range of service and comfort to the traveling public. Flying today is not only safe and efficient, it is comfortable and can be quite relaxing."

Bob Blattmer
Director, Public Relations
Trans World Airlines

In a hurry? If you are and can afford it, the European Concorde is the fastest commercial aircraft currently available. The Concorde is a supersonic transport (SST). SST's can fly at speeds over fifteen hundred miles per hour—that's more than twice the speed of sound. That means that in an SST you could fly from New York to London in only three hours.

In-Flight Service

There are basically two classes of service, first class and coach.

First-class service provides more comfortable seats, no crowds, excellent meals with a choice of entrees, and free drinks. First-class passengers usually board and deplane first and receive superior flight service.

For people who are afraid or simply do not like to fly, paying extra for a first-class ticket might be worth the money. If you don't like crowds and the flight is full, you might be wise to travel in first class. I've known quite a few people who are very uncomfortable and nervous when crowded onto a full plane, but who can easily relax and enjoy the flight if they travel in first class. It's more expensive. However, if flying in first class makes the difference between going or not going, then it's money well spent.

Special Services

Every airline offers special services that cater to passengers' particular needs. You can request a salt-free or kosher meal; you can arrange to borrow a wheelchair or a pet carrier. If you have a child, most airlines will assist you by warming a baby bottle or keeping an eye on your unaccompanied child.

Anyone with a physical handicap or limitation should inquire about the availability of special services either through a travel agent or directly with the airlines.

If you are traveling with a child who is afraid to fly, the airline can help. Pilots frequently invite children into the cockpit before or after a flight; a stewardess can arrange the visit. Airline personnel can answer technical questions the child may have. Children who are afraid of flying can usually overcome their fears with some patient listening by an adult and a clear explanation of what is going on. It is important that children, as all of us, not be degraded or made to feel ashamed of their fears. Acceptance will do wonders. It is also a good idea to bring something to amuse children during the flight.

Seating

Seating is important to many passengers, including me. This can be especially important on crowded flights. Airline reservation agents and travel agents can help passengers select the seat they want in advance.

Some people like window seats, some people like seats near the door, still others prefer to sit over the wings. With an aisle seat, you will have better legroom and it is easier to get in and out. Most planes offer smoking and non-smoking sections. An early reservation will ensure you the seat you prefer. If an airline reservationist or travel agent doesn't ask you, tell him you would like advance seat selection.

Airports

There are more than thirteen thousand airports in the United States. Most of these are only for small airplanes. Scheduled air carriers serve about five hundred airports. Most cities have at least one good-sized airport. Cities the size of New York or Chicago will have as many as thirty airports serving the city and its suburbs. Chicago's O'Hare Airport is the busiest airport in the world, with nearly two thousand flights each day.

Most flights are to and from large, complex airports. Large airports can be frustrating, confusing, and stressful. When it comes to flying, the first obstacle is simply getting to the airport. Major airports seem always to be located across town and where the traffic is nearly impossible. Major airports seem almost always to be crowded. If you have a small airport near you, sometimes called a satellite airport, you may be able to save yourself a lot of headaches.

Regardless of the airport you choose, getting to the airport and parking will probably still be a hassle. Usually bus, limousine, and taxi services are available. Considering the cost of parking and the frustration of traffic jams, using public transportation is a good alternative. If you drive your own car, you may be forced to park miles away from the airport, so you end up with a bus ride anyway.

Consider the time of day you plan to travel. To get to a major airport at rush hour is next to impossible. It is not uncommon for the trip to the airport, parking, and checking baggage to take longer than the flight.

Once at the airport, you are faced with trying to figure out what is where. As we will discuss later, a trial run to the airport can eliminate a lot of anxiety and provide you with a good idea of what you will need to do and where you need to do it. If you are especially apprehensive, I strongly recommend that you take that trial run to your airport prior to flying. Some airports have excellent restaurants with a view of the planes arriving and departing. Going to the airport ahead of time is a good way to familiarize yourself with airplanes and airports.

On the positive side, airports are alive and pulsating. With the right attitude, the hustle and bustle can be transformed into a dynamic and exciting event. The main thing is not to be in a hurry. Give yourself a lot of extra time.

After arriving at the airport and finding your way to the air carrier you will be flying with, the next step is to take care of your baggage. Anything carried on the plane must fit completely underneath your seat. Generally speaking, you can take one piece of hand-carried luggage the size of a large attaché case or makeup bag. If not too large, many airlines will allow you to hand carry a suit bag aboard.

A good rule of thumb is to pack light. If you can avoid checking any baggage, you get to skip a few obstacles. If you do check baggage, always look at the baggage tag to make sure it's properly labeled. It's also a good idea to have your name and address inside your bag.

Here are some ways to make your time in an airport as comfortable as possible:

- Have advance reservations, tickets, and seat selection.
- Use a satellite airport.
- Travel at an uncrowded time.
- Avoid checking baggage.
- Get to the airport early.

Once at the airport, you will be directed by airline personnel to the boarding area or gate. This is where you check in and receive a boarding pass. Somewhere along the way you will pass through an X-ray device. This is another safety feature to ensure no one carries a weapon aboard the plane.

Some Friendly Recommendations

For people who have never flown, here are some friendly recommendations:

- Start with a short flight—less than one hour.
- Fly on a jet.
- Fly during fair weather.
- Give yourself lots of time—don't hurry.
- Schedule the trip to a place you want to go.
- No business meetings, children, or other outside pressures.
- Buy your ticket in advance.
- If it is available, go/select/try First Class on your first flight.
- Travel with a friend who understands the situation.
- Avoid crowded airports and airplanes.

3
THE FLIGHT

"Ladies and gentlemen, Flight 45 to Atlanta, Georgia, is now boarding at Gate Number 11. Please present your boarding pass to the flight attendant aboard the plane."

Once you are aboard the airplane and have found your seat, you will notice a fresh-air vent above your head. Reach up and adjust it—fresh air will make you more comfortable. As we will cover later, this is a key time. Don't tense up and immobilize yourself.

When the airplane is ready, the engines will be started. Jet planes are quiet; you'll probably not notice any engine noise. Propeller engines are a bit noisy—plus, of course, you can see the propeller spinning. The pilot will call the airport tower by radio and request permission to taxi to the runway for takeoff. You'll be advised of this by the stewards or stewardesses:

"Fasten your seat belts, no smoking, and please check to ensure your seat backs and tray tables are in their upright position."

You will also hear a brief safety talk, telling you where the safety exits are, where the life jackets are if the flight is over water, and what to do in case of cabin depressurization.

What in the world is cabin depressurization? It is really simple to understand. When you're on the ground you breathe air containing a certain amount of oxygen, depending on the altitude. For your comfort, airliner cabins are sealed and pressurized. Having a pressurized cabin means that even if you fly at thirty thousand feet, you will feel the same and get approximately the same amount of oxygen as you did when you were on the ground. If in a freak accident the cabin loses its pressure (cabin depressurization), you would want to breathe supplemental oxygen until the captain takes the plane down to a more comfortable altitude.

Don't ignore or hide from information because thinking about those things makes you uncomfortable. The more informed you are, the more capable you are to take charge of your life.

What Will Happen

The captain will taxi to the runway and radio the airport tower requesting permission to depart. The captain will ring a bell to let the cabin crew know all is ready to go.

The captain will then smoothly accelerate the plane down the runway. When the pressure above the wings decreases sufficiently the plane will gently lift off the ground. Different planes lift off the ground at different speeds. Small planes lift off at around 70 miles per hour. Most commercial jets lift off the ground at around 120 miles per hour.

Once airborne the next sound you'll hear, if you listen closely, is the landing gear being retracted. The captain will gradually increase the altitude to a predetermined level to provide for the smoothest and fastest trip. The captain climbs at around five hundred to a thousand feet per minute; it's a lot like going up in an elevator. A slow and gentle increase in altitude is used because it is easier on you, the passenger.

About five to ten minutes after takeoff, the captain will ring the bell again. This bell lets the cabin crew know that they may now move about the cabin and begin their job of making your flight comfortable and enjoyable. Use the sound of this bell as a cue to stretch, take a deep breath, and relax.

You cannot be scared and relaxed at the same time. It is physiologically impossible.

The captain will then turn off the seat belt sign, indicating that passengers may now get up and move about the cabin. If you feel up to it, I highly recommend standing and stretching or taking a walk down the aisle.

Your seat is adjustable, you have a tray for drinks or cards, you have a reading light, a fresh-air vent, and a button to call the flight attendant.

Remember, throughout the flight the captain is in constant radio contact with the ground. The plane is also continuously monitored on radar by air-traffic controllers.

Airline captains are required to make all flight maneuvers gently. You do not need to worry that the plane is going to lean way over or descend quickly.

"The FAA requires all commercial carriers to make their turns at a standard rate of one degree per 1.5 seconds. At this rate, it takes four minutes for a 360-degree turn. Imagine taking four minutes to turn your car in a circle. This is very gentle . . . at this rate it is difficult to tell you are changing direction."

> Richard Cox
> Chief, Los Angeles Approach Control
> Federal Aviation Administration

You will probably never even notice when the captain starts descending. The gradual descent for landing may begin hundreds of miles before reaching the destination. Unless you are watching the clock, you probably won't know that you are about to arrive until you hear the arrival announcement.

"Ladies and gentlemen, we will be arriving in a few minutes. Please be sure your seat backs and tray tables are in the upright position. Please fasten your seat belt. No smoking until inside the terminal area. Thank you for flying with us. We hope your flight was enjoyable and we'll be seeing you again soon."

As you near the ground, the captain lowers the landing gear. Again, this is a humming sound that lasts about five seconds. The captain will ring a bell to let the crew know it is time for them to be seated for landing. Also, the captain will lower the flaps. Flaps are the rear part of the wing and are used to allow the plane to fly slower.

Most landings are so gentle it is difficult to tell when the wheels actually touch the ground. Just before the wheels touch, the captain will add power to keep the airplane stable. To slow the plane, once on the ground, the captain reverses the engines. As mentioned earlier, the engines are really not reversed. Actually, the engine's exhaust, is deflected to help slow the plane.

Of course you don't need to be an expert on flying to be a comfortable passenger. I am suggesting that the more you understand, the easier it will be for you to relax and enjoy your flying experience.

Turbulence

A few years ago I was a passenger leaving Reno, Nevada, en route to Los Angeles. It was a stormy day, gray and very windy. After sitting down, I looked around the plane and noticed a number of people seemed apprehensive. As we taxied to the runway, it started to snow. The airport in Reno is situated next to some large mountains. It was a scary situation—flying in the snow and near the mountains.

The usual departure announcements were given and two bells rang, signaling the cabin crew of our departure. As the plane lifted from the runway, it really jolted around. Here was a situation that could permanently turn someone against flying.

The advantage I had over some of the other passengers was that I knew what was happening—and what to expect. Just like the crew and many other experienced passengers, I knew there was no real reason to be afraid. Sure you might still feel scared. But, if you know what to expect, your fear will be less, and it will be much more manageable.

First, snow does not affect the operation of the airplane or the engines. The wind and the mountains are going to make the plane bounce around. However, I knew the bouncing would stop a few minutes after departure when the plane gained altitude. I also knew that we would soon be flying above the clouds and into the sunshine.

If you're flying along and it gets bumpy, you are either crossing mountains, flying through some weather, or the air is being moved by a temperature change. Remember your high school physics class—hot air rises. Unless the turbulence is very minor or going to last just a few minutes, the airline captain will change altitude and return to smooth air. Airline pilots are sensitive to passengers' concern caused by turbulence and do their best to provide a smooth flight.

"I believe most airline captains feel as I do and are very conscious that they are carrying passengers. All our flight maneuvers are done gently. We work to en-

34

sure that each flight is as smooth as possible.

"I wish there were some way to convey to the passengers how really safe flying is. If you were to fly eight hours every day you could fly for two hundred years before the odds were against you."

Captain Bill Thomas
Pilot
USAir

The days of getting airsick are all but gone. If you are especially concerned about getting airsick, you might try one of the commercial motion-sickness pills. It really isn't necessary, but if it makes you feel more confident, that's reason enough.

What if it is very windy when it's time for your flight? Will you have a rough flight? Will it be safe?

Think of this. We know that planes are designed to be flown in the air. Even the slowest plane flies at speeds over one hundred miles per hour. That means that the slowest plane is designed to operate in at least a hundred-mile-per-hour wind! A very windy day—with winds of twenty to thirty miles per hour—presents no problem for something that was built to fly.

So, if it's windy on the day of your flight, the takeoff and landing might be a little bumpy. If you're crossing mountains, there may be a bump or two. And if the air temperature is changing, you might experience some turbulence. Turbulence is a lot like driving down a dirt road; it's not dangerous, just bumpy.

Enough about weather. Here are the important things for you to remember about turbulence:

- Just because the weather where you are leaving from is crummy, that doesn't mean it will be crummy where you land.
- Airplanes are designed and well equipped to fly in all kinds of weather. (Weather bureau planes fly into hurricanes to check the size of the storm.)
- Airplanes fly above most weather.

Flying at Night

Is flying at night any different from flying during the day? From a pilot's point of view—no, not really. The differences are about the same as the differences between day and night driving. Statistically, flying is just as safe at night as it is in the day.

For the passenger, flying at night can be a good idea. Airports and airplanes are often less crowded at night. Also, late-night flights can be real money savers. With the plane less than full, you will have a better choice of seating, quicker in-flight service, and probably even an empty seat next to you so you can stretch out and be more comfortable. Most people sleep on long night flights.

Some people are bothered more if there is turbulence at night since they can't see why the plane is bouncing around. If this is the case, ask a crew member who can check with the pilot to let you know what's causing the turbulence and how long it will last. By the way, night flights are generally smoother than day flights because the air is likely to be more stable. In the daytime, the sun heats the air, causing it to rise and creating turbulence.

Of course, the choice is yours. If you don't like flying at night, don't. If you prefer night flying, then pick a night flight whenever convenient. On long trips, I personally prefer to fly at night so I can pass the time by sleeping.

Back on the Ground

In the terminal you'll first have to collect your luggage. The luggage area or the incoming gate is a common place to have your friends or relatives meet you.

All major air terminals have bus, taxi, and rent-a-car services. If you are going to a hotel near the airport, there is probably free shuttle service available. Throughout most air terminals there are free courtesy telephones. If you have any questions, simply pick up any courtesy phone and help is at hand.

4
WHAT IS FEAR?

Now that we have a basic understanding of flying, let's focus on our fears, find out what they are, and learn how to handle them.

First and very important, please understand that fear is a normal and fairly common emotion. Sure, it's not a favorite. But certain situations are going to make you scared. Fear also has a positive side. Fear alerts us to dangers and, as such, is not something that we would want to ignore.

Fear can be experienced in many ways and be associated with almost anything—real or imagined. It is only human to be afraid at times. Being afraid is a normal psychological process—a part of life.

We need to recognize that fear can be realistic or unrealistic. How we react to fear can be either normal or exaggerated.

To experience fear is one thing. Letting fear control your life is something to avoid. It has been my experience that most people have little trouble handling fear in its milder forms—say, a job interview or a scary movie. Even though none of us are completely comfortable with these experiences, they don't usually produce too much anxiety and can even be exciting and fun.

Unrealistic fears are fears based upon things that are imaginary. By imaginary I mean most people would agree that the thing feared is not really a potential hazard. An example of an unrealistic fear is being afraid to go outside when the moon is full.

If you don't understand something, such as flying, then your fear is often a fear of the unknown. Fear of the unknown can be realistic or unrealistic depending on what it is that you are afraid of. The more you learn about something, the more realistic you can be in assessing whether there is any real danger.

For the many people who have a difficult time when it comes to flying, their fear is often exaggerated—full of seemingly unbearable anxiety. During an anxiety attack, normal bodily reactions are overstimulated and the results can be devastating.

Phobias

Let's clear up some common misunderstandings about phobias. A phobia, from the Greek word *phobos*, which means "to flee," is a situation in which there is a great deal of fear caused by a particular event or thing. If someone is truly phobic about something, it is evident in his or her reactions to that particular situation. The intensity of fear and anxiety will be severe. The phobic person feels a very strong need to get away from the situation.

A phobia might be based on something that presents some real danger, like lightning, or it could be based on something totally unrealistic. If the reaction to that real or imagined danger is overly strong, and there is an excessive amount of anxiety, then the person can be considered phobic.

People can be phobic about almost anything—dirt (mysophobia), water (hydrophobia), thunder (keraunophobia), snakes (ophidiophobia), flowers (antrophobia), and flying (aviophobia). The American Psychological Association lists 220 phobias. There is even phobiaphobia—fear of having a phobia. The world's most common phobia is agoraphobia. Agoraphobia is a fear of leaving the house or neighborhood. Fear of heights (acrophobia), of closed-in spaces (claustrophobia), fear of crowds (ochlophobia) and of darkness (nyctophobia) are other common phobias. Being phobic about something does not mean someone is mentally ill. It does mean that things have gotten out of hand and professional help might be a good idea.

There is not a clear understanding of why some people become phobic and others experience no reaction at all to the same event. Some psychologists and psychiatrists will argue that phobias are deeply rooted in one's childhood. Maybe this is true and maybe it isn't. What we do know is that a phobic reaction is usually very intense and can severely limit a person's ability to enjoy life. Understanding what started a phobia will not relieve the panic, confusion, or anxiety. Understanding alone will not give you an effective method to handle fear, panic, and anxiety. What is needed is a practical, workable approach to handling your fears.

How Nerves Work

Let's take a look at how our nervous system works so we can understand how to control our nervous reactions.

There is no mystery about how nerves work. Our nervous system works in two ways. Some of our nerves and muscles are controlled voluntarily—such as those in our hands and legs. Other nerves do not need our direction to function—such as those in our heart and lungs. These nerves are called involuntary, or autonomic. Emotions activate both our voluntary and our involuntary nervous systems.

You can control your voluntary nerves just by telling yourself to relax. Once you are aware that you are tensing voluntary muscle groups, you can relax them through conscious control. Involuntary nerves are more difficult to control. You must be patient with involuntary nerves; they take longer to relax because involuntary nerves are not under your immediate conscious control. Tense involuntary nerves are similar to a bad habit—and as with a bad habit, they take time to change. If you keep relaxing your voluntary muscles, your involuntary muscles will also relax.

If your nerves overreact, meaning that you get tenser than the situation warrants, this indicates that your nerves have become overly sensitive. Your nerves have developed a hair trigger. You see, nerves and muscles become conditioned to respond in certain ways. Each time you respond, or overrespond, you are conditioning yourself. Rather than learning to relax, many of us unknowingly learn to become tense.

Anxiety is the psychological state characterized by apprehensiveness and tension. When we are confronted with a situation that we don't want to experience, we resist by physically tensing our muscles and restricting our breathing. We can easily become conditioned to tense up at the very first sign that something unpleasant might happen. And, the more you avoid, the more you tense up. The more you tense up and avoid, the more you are conditioning your nerves to become overly sensitive. It's a vicious cycle.

So, fear of flying is really a question of how sensitive your nerves are and how much extra stress flying adds to your life. You could be bored with flying and have no involuntary stress reaction or anxiety. You could be excited about flying—moderate involuntary reactions. You could be afraid—a lot of involuntary nerve activity and anxiety. You could have a flying phobia—exaggerated involuntary reaction from your overly sensitive nerves.

Try to remember two basic facts:
• Anyone can become sensitized to anything.
• Anyone can become desensitized to anything.
Sometimes sensitization happens rapidly and traumatically. An example of this might be a phobia of winding roads developing after an au-

tomobile accident in the mountains. Each time this person gets on a winding road, he fears a reoccurrence of the accident. If not handled properly, this type of fear could develop into a fear of cars and eventually severely limit this person's life.

More often sensitization comes about gradually and is not directly related to a specific event or thing. If we are under stress for long periods of time, then it is likely we will develop overly sensitive nerves. Overly sensitive nerves can put us in a position where, when stress is increased even just a little, *whamo*, we have a full-blown anxiety attack. And yes—flying, traveling, packing, moving, airports, parking, waiting in lines, and unfamiliar surroundings are all potentially stressful situations. It is easy to see that the person with a "fear of flying" might really just be an overstressed individual who hasn't learned how to handle the extra stress of an airplane trip.

As you might have guessed, when stress is relieved, the nerves will settle down. Without stress, many phobias simply dissipate or their sources turn into things we simply don't like to do. And it *is* possible to do something you don't like and not be anxious about it.

The vast majority of people who have a difficult time when it comes to flying are not nervously ill. They are, however, suffering from an overreaction to an experience they perceive as fearful. Again, it is important to recognize that fear is normal and needn't be avoided. The overreactions do need control—but avoiding fearful events is not the answer. Many people act as if they've never been afraid. Many people deny, hide, and avoid fear. But fear is a part of life. It is okay to be fearful at times.

The problem isn't the fear, the problem is the overreaction.

Under normal circumstances if something scares us, then we experience that fear directly and that's that. It was scary and it's over. Our reactions were normal and didn't linger. As already mentioned, without *over*reactions, fear can even be exciting. Think how many scary things—such as horror movies or starting a new job—can be exciting as long as the fear doesn't get out of hand.

You're okay as long as you don't panic.

Fear-Tension Cycle

For the fearful flyer, what we have then is a case of involuntary overreactions of varying severity related in some way to flying. The initial fear has, for the fearful flyer, simply gotten out of hand. Instead of just experiencing fear directly, the fear is increased by the additional stress of trying to figure out what is wrong and trying to stop the experience. The more a person struggles not to experience some experience, the more stress is added. The more stress, the more reactions—the more reactions, the more stress, often ending in a case of panic.

Let me give you an example. A passenger—let's call him Tom—is flying along one night and all of a sudden a flash of lightning illuminates the evening sky. Everyone on the plane is startled, momentarily scared. However, Tom wants to avoid the feeling of fear and says to himself, "What if the lightning hits the plane?" Tom closes his eyes tightly. His breathing becomes constricted, and his mind starts repeating, "I gotta get out of here." The cycle has begun: fear, tension, more fear, more tension. Tom is becoming increasingly nervous. He is confused and thinks he is afraid of lightning. The fear is not of the lightning. It is the fear of the panic that follows the overreaction to the initial experience.

Everyone has certain things or events that are likely to set off that vicious fear-tension cycle. And, as mentioned, flying is a common one. These things or events that set off our nervous reactions are called *cues*. The severity of our reactions will vary depending on how sensitized our nerves are.

When someone remarks that he or she is afraid to fly, we really don't know much about that fear—only that there is probably a nervous overreaction that is in some way associated with the event of flying. The source of that fear could be closed spaces, lack of control, fear of dizziness, fear of heights, and so on.

To effectively handle fear of flying, it is necessary to identify fear cues and set about to break up the fear-tension cycle. I don't mean eliminate fear, though many fearful fliers have become avid travelers. The object is to decrease the intensity of your fear and make you less susceptible to tension and anxiety when flying.

We need to experience fear without overreacting or trying to avoid the experience. The result will be more self-control and confidence as you learn that you can handle comfortably any obstacle that may get in your way.

You can learn to face, modify, and change fears.

5
IDENTIFYING YOUR FEARS

To develop an effective Fear Recovery Program, it is necessary to identify exactly what causes you to become anxious. Let's take a look at some of the facts about aviophobia—its causes and cures.

Developing Aviophobia

What causes one person to develop a fear of flying while another person develops a love of flying?

Most cases of aviophobia develop between the ages of twenty and thirty-five. Aviophobia has no relationship to sex, education, occupation, religion, or race. Women are more than twice as likely to admit to being afraid and seek professional help. According to Pan American Airways' Captain T. W. "Slim" Cummings, fear of flying is a common problem affecting an estimated twenty-five million Americans. Althought there are no firm statistics, people all over the world appear to have just as many problems getting on airplanes as do Americans.

There is definitely a relationship between the amount of stress in a person's life and the onset of a fear of flying. In the vast majority of reported cases, and in every case I have personally dealt with, there was a high level of stress in the person's life at the time the fear of flying developed. People under chronic (long-term) stress are the most prone to developing phobias, such as fear of flying.

Some people who shake at the thought of flying have never flown. Some people develop their fear after one flight, while others start becoming afraid after many years of flying comfortably. It appears that stress is the major contributing factor to the development of aviophobia.

There are cases of people who, though they have flown comfortably for years, all of a sudden and with no apparent cause have developed a severe fear of flying.

"I had been working for the airlines for ten or eleven years. I normally flew on business trips, say four or five times a month. My wife and I would fly somewhere probably once a month for short weekend getaways. I had always liked to fly—that's probably the biggest reason I was working for an airline. Mostly flying was routine.

"Then one day as I was boarding the plane, I felt gloomy—somehow like I shouldn't go on this flight. I went ahead aboard anyway and was pretty shaken by the time the flight was over. I just didn't want to fly anymore.

"I guess it lasted three or four months. I even thought of quitting my job. It was crazy. And then, just as quickly as it came, the fear was gone. I still don't understand what happened."

Dick Beaulleau
Sales Manager
Continental Airlines

If someone has a bad experience when flying—for example, an exceptionally turbulent flight or a near accident—he may begin to think flying really is dangerous. However, a "bad flight," in and of itself, doesn't mean that someone will develop a fear of flying. According to studies reported in the *American Journal of Psychiatry*, the majority of people who have been in an actual plane crash don't develop aviophobia and successfully return to flying.

Even pilots can develop a sudden fear of flying. Again, the onset seems related more to stress than to any single event. Research outlined in the *American Journal of Psychotherapy* and the *British Journal of Psychiatry* indicates that 83 percent of the people who seek professional help are able to significantly reduce or completely eliminate fear associated with flying.

The most successful form of therapy for curing a flying phobia is the one that uses positive conditioning and stress-resolution techniques. Group psychotherapy and psychoanalysis, unless combined with behavioral techniques, prove largely ineffective as a cure for aviophobia.

Learning to Be Afraid

Unfortunately, most of what we hear about airlines and flying is negative. All of this negative conditioning can convince us that flying isn't safe and helps some people justify their fear of flying.

We don't see headlines reading:

FUN IN FLIGHT
THIS YEAR OVER A MILLION PEOPLE FLY
SAFELY TO HAWAII FOR VACATION

With all the misleading information, even if we don't become convinced that flying is dangerous, we still can end up with the opinion that flying is something we should avoid.

Being afraid doesn't mean that you are phobic. Remember, a phobia is an overreaction. Of the many people who say they have a flying phobia, undoubtedly many simply don't like to fly. They are not really phobic about flying.

We can learn to be afraid of flying by reading, watching, and hearing about air disasters. If an airplane crashes, it is front-page news. Newspapers frequently run feature articles on the danger of flying.

> "Planes Flying Higher Invite Disaster"
> —*Los Angeles Times*

Then there are the many magazines and books telling of the horrors of flying.

"The World's Most Dangerous Airports"
— *Cosmopolitan*

"Fire in Flight"
— *Reader's Digest*

Let's not forget what we learn watching movies and television. What child hasn't seen a war movie of airplanes burning and exploding or movies in which an airplane crashes into the sea or a jungle full of prehistoric beasts? Add to this newscasts of actual disasters and the conditioning process is almost overwhelming.

Airport: a crazy passenger takes a bomb and explodes it on board as a snowstorm covers the runway.

Airport 1978: a midair collision between a light aircraft and a jumbo jet kills the crew, and the stewardess must fly the plane.

Airplane: food poisoning, and the crew can't fly, so a former jet jockey must try to make an emergency landing—of course, the weather is terrible.

Airport 1980: a jumbo jet crashes into the sea and sinks with the passengers alive and trapped.

Recovery

A person who has never or seldom flown and fears flying is more likely to completely lose his fear of flying than someone who has flown a lot and still fears flying.

Just as quickly as some phobias develop, some disappear.

Recall a common childhood fear, say darkness. As you grew older the fear disappeared, right? Let me explain what happened. The fear didn't just vanish by magic. What happened was that as you grew older you learned more. Gradually and progressively, you learned how to become increasingly relaxed in dark places. If you are relaxed you cannot be afraid.

This is a very important point. If you can relax, you can control and eliminate fear. You can't physiologically or psychologically be relaxed and scared at the same time.

When flying, if your fears don't diminish, it is because you are staying tense as you fly. And, if you are tense when you fly, you are conditioning, teaching, and reinforcing yourself to fear flying.

Another major point to remember is that it is not necessary to discover the reason you become afraid in order to be cured. As a matter of fact, looking for the reason you're afraid is a trap because it allows you to justify and avoid dealing with your fear.

The key question to ask is not, "Why am I afraid?" The key question to ask is, "What am I going to do about my fear?"

Questions and Answers

As a therapist and lecturer on flying and psychology, I frequently get questions about fears and phobias. Here are some common questions and answers:

Q. Are fears inherited?

A. Most all fears are learned. Fears of such

things as fire, drowning, or heights might have some primordial biological or survival function, but even as instincts these fears are conditionable. By conditionable I mean that we can learn to control our instincts. Just because you are afraid of water doesn't mean you can't learn to swim.

Q. Does having a phobia mean you have a physical problem or disease?

A. No, not at all. Phobias can and do affect healthy and unhealthy people. People with a fear-of-flying phobia do not have hypoglycemia, epilepsy, a weak heart, or a brain tumor. The keys to developing a phobia are past life experiences, conditioning, and stress.

Q. But doesn't stress cause physical problems?

A. Yes, stress is a factor in a number of physical problems. But stress causes the illness, the phobia doesn't. If you fear elephants and never go to the zoo, your elephant phobia won't provide any stress. No elephants, no stress.

Q. You said that during an anxiety attack, people panic and think they will collapse, vomit, or go crazy. Is this really true?

A. Sure—the key word here is *think*. People may think they will pass out or freak out. They won't. The mind is just working overtime. What we think is going to happen and what really happens are usually quite different.

Q. Can everyone recover from fear of flying?

A. *Recover* is a difficult word. Get better or improve, yes. I think this is possible for everyone. Certain types of people don't recover as well as others.

nat types?

It is not a good idea to categorize people. But to answer your question, let me say that three types of personalities are slow to recover from a phobia.

Type 1 is the generally overtense person; you know, the perfectionist type.

Type 2 is the person preoccupied with his or her bodily sensations. These people tend to dwell on their feelings too much. Paying too much attention to *you* accentuates the problem and slows recovery.

Type 3 is the unassertive, accepter person. This person makes little effort. "If this is my fate, what can I do?" These people are the most discouraging to work with. Basically, you must want to get over your fears or not much can be done.

Q. What do you do if you do get scared and panic?

A. Don't fight it. As difficult as it sounds, each of us must accept all of our experiences—even panic.

Q. Are you suggesting people not try to avoid panic? When panic gets me, it's more than I can handle.

A. First, panic doesn't just happen. Though you probably feel you're a victim of circumstances, you aren't. Panic always requires some input from the victim. What we say to ourselves will make the difference between panic and just becoming temporarily uncomfortable. Second—and this is a very important point—panic starts out at the worst it's going to get. Once you feel it, the worst is over.

Q. Please explain what you mean by the worst is over?

A. When we come up against something fearful, we tense ourselves and our body produces adrenaline. This adrenaline is to help us survive—flee or fight danger. Now, your body doesn't know the difference between an attacking tiger and a learned fear like flying. Your body reacts the same. If you're scared you are going to get a shot of adrenaline. The body operates mechanically and has a limited supply of adrenaline. Your body can't continue to supply adrenaline. You get the worst first. It's like what you feel if you have a near auto accident. Adrenaline makes your heart race and maybe you get sweaty and cold. The point is— once you have received the shot of adrenaline, it's not going to get worse.

Q. I'm very scared of dogs. I think the word is *cynophobic*. How can I find out why I have this fear?

A. There are a number of ways. Psychoanalysis, certain forms of counseling, hypnosis, or you could ask your parents. But it doesn't matter if you never find out, except for your own curiosity. Please understand this. Knowing or not knowing the cause of a phobia makes no difference with respect to cure or recovery.

Q. Are phobias dangerous?

A. No. The stress produced can cause or contribute to physical problems, and irrational thinking could get someone into trouble. But phobias themselves—they're scary, inconvenient, and frustrating. They are not dangerous.

Agoraphobia

As mentioned earlier, when a person says he is afraid to fly, he really hasn't said exactly what frightens him. Some people may be afraid of heights while others may panic when enclosed in small spaces. Motion, speed, darkness, or some other fear may be the real culprit when someone says he is afraid to fly.

By far the most common phobia underlying a fear of flying is agoraphobia. Literally, *agoraphobia* means "fear of the marketplace." Actually, agoraphobia is a fear of traveling away from the security of the home. The feeling of being in a place where help is not readily available, or of being "bugged" in crowded places away from home, is likely an agoraphobic reaction. People who feel they must sit in the aisle at the movies or near the door at meetings or who say they just "don't like travel" are often suffering from agoraphobia.

Often related to what psychology calls *separation anxiety*, agoraphobia is one of the most common phobias. Some psychologists estimate that as many as one out of every five people will suffer symptoms of agoraphobia sometime during his life. The main difference between agoraphobia and other phobic reactions is that agoraphobia is more of an internal feeling than a fear of some specific object or circumstance.

It is again important to remember that whatever the phobia and regardless of the cause, the treatment remains the same.

Also it is important not to get caught up in labeling yourself or others. If you call yourself weak or shy or phobic, then you are reinforcing these ideas and feelings about yourself. It is a lot easier to recover from being uncomfortable than from being phobic.

Find and use a substitute word for *phobia* and *fear*. I like the word *uptight*. Just listen to the difference: "I have a flying phobia." "I get uptight flying." The first statement sounds as if the person needs professional help. The second describes a normal person who simply doesn't like to fly. Words can make a difference.

First and Second Fears

When you are startled at a horror movie or by screeching brakes, you experience fear. As we've discussed, this is normal. Even though many people may be reluctant to admit it, everyone feels fear. Adrenaline might give us a momentary shaky feeling and pounding heart, but once the danger or imagined danger has passed, we settle down and return to our usual selves. This type of fear is called *first fear*.

If we have oversensitized nerves or overreact to a first fear, we have what is called *second fear*. Second fear is the key that keeps people locked in that vicious cycle. Dr. Albert Ellis calls the process of giving ourselves second fear *catastrophizing*. Catastrophizing is when we add catastrophic and scary thoughts to the first fear. For example, if you are flying in an airplane and the plane encounters some turbulence, this turbulence could produce a first fear. If you say to yourself, "I can't take this," or

"I'm going to get airsick," you are catastrophizing and producing a second fear.

It is absolutely essential that you learn not to compound a first fear with a second fear. When you are scared, be scared. The first step in getting control over your fear is to stop making what scares you worse—and that means stopping the second fear. Each time you can control a fear, you get stronger.

Getting Control

Controlling fear is quite simple—though not necessarily easy. It's a lot like quitting smoking:

- You know you probably should do it.
- It's easier for some people than others.
- Motivation is important.
- It is a personal matter.
- A lot of people will give you advice.
- Some people won't understand your struggle.
- The best time to start is when you are ready.
- Only you can do it.
- It can be done.

Habits

Being afraid of certain things is often just a habit. Sounds simple—and it is. As we grow up, we experience many things. Some things frighten us, some don't. As we get older and gain more knowledge and experience, a lot of our childhood fears disappear. Some fears linger on, and if the fear hangs around long enough, it can become a habit. Throw in some stress, exaggerate your fear with a second fear, and you've turned your fear into a phobia.

Imagine a person whose first few flights were scary. Add to those scary flights the negative conditioning that comes from newspapers and movies, couple this with the unfamiliarity of the airport, add some stress, and it's easy to see how these circumstances might get out of control. If this fear is not dealt with effectively, this person could easily develop a habit of being afraid of flying. People can, and often do, get used to being afraid. Ask yourself—are you still really scared or is your fear just a habit?

Cues

Being afraid is personal. What scares one person may not bother another. In order to recover from your fears, you will need to identify exactly what makes you uncomfortable.

Some people might shake at the thought of going up in a small plane, while others might like small planes but think flying over mountains is the really scary part.

I suggest anyone wanting to lessen or eliminate his or her fear of flying fill out this questionnaire. Even if you are comfortable flying, I think you'll find the results interesting. Just write in the book.

1. Do you consider yourself to have a fear of flying?
   ☐ No
   ☒ Yes

2. What are your feelings about flying?
   ☒ Terrified
   ☐ Don't like the thought/idea
   ☐ It's okay
   ☐ Mostly enjoyable
   ☐ Love it

3. Have you ever flown?
   ☐ No
   ☒ Yes. Approximately how many times?
   _10_

4. What type(s) of airplane have you flown in?
   ☐ None
   ☐ Small private plane
   ☒ Propeller passenger plane
   ☒ Medium-sized jet
   ☒ Jumbo or wide-body jet

5. Were either of your parents afraid to fly?
   ☐ No
   ☒ Yes
   ☐ Don't know

6. Are you afraid of heights, small places, crowds, being confined, or leaving home?
   ☐ No
   ☐ Yes. List your fears: _Heights,_
   small places, crowds,
   being confined, heights

7. What is the most frightening thing about flying for you?

Taking oFF, Torbulence

8. When you see or read about a plane crash, what is your reaction?
   ☒ Makes me even more scared
   ☐ Confirms my fears
   ☐ Interested but no real emotional response
   ☐ No interest

9. Are you now, or are you usually, under a lot of stress?
   ☐ No
   ☒ Yes

10. Describe the worst thing that could happen to you on an airplane. _Faint,_
    panic, Die

11. When you get scared, what happens to you?
    ☒ Tense all over
    ☒ Weak legs
    ☐ Headache
    ☐ Nausea
    ☒ Hands shake
    ☐ Difficulty in breathing
    ☒ Restless
    ☒ Irritable
    ☐ Hysterical
    ☐ Strange thoughts
    ☒ Can't concentrate
    ☒ Dizziness
    ☐ Heart palpitations
    ☐ Cold hands

☒ Sweat
☐ Blushing
☐ Feel encapsulated
☐ Other. Describe your reactions: _____

---

12. What do you usually do when you fly?
    ☒ Read
    ☐ Look out the window
    ☐ Drink
    ☒ Think
    ☒ Talk with other people
    ☐ Play a game
    ☐ Other. Describe: _____

---

13. Would you rather travel _____?
    ☐ Alone
    ☒ With a good friend
    ☐ With husband or wife

14. Is your fear of flying a secret?
    ☒ No
    ☐ Yes

15. Rate your self-esteem (feelings about yourself)
    ☐ I think I'm special
    ☐ I'm better than average
    ☐ I'm average
    ☒ I'm not okay

16. Do you eat when flying?
    ☐ No
    ☒ Yes

17. Do you take anything to help you fly?
    ☐ No
    ☒ Yes. ☒ Booze

☐ Sleeping pills
☐ Motion-sickness pills
☐ Tranquilizers
☐ Other. List: _____

18. Rate the following according to how much they frighten you:

1 = Very much
2 = Some
3 = Not at all

*1*__ Why I am traveling
*2*__ Whom I am traveling with
*2*__ Destination
*1*__ Length of flight
*2*__ Time of departure
*1*__ Weather
*1*__ Mountains
*1*__ Type of plane
*1*__ Size of plane
*1*__ Sitting in smoking (or no-smoking) section
*1*__ Where I sit
*2*__ Crowds
*1*__ Noise
*3*__ The doors closing
*1*__ Movement of plane
*1*__ Takeoff
*2*__ Being enclosed
*3*__ Height of the flight
*1*__ Turbulence
*1*__ Plane changing direction
*2*__ Having other people sit next to me
*1*__ Location of rest rooms
*2*__ Other people bothering me
*2*__ Inability to move around
*2*__ Landing

19. What have you done or could you do to make flying less stressful for you?

- ☒ Fly only on certain types of airplanes
- ☐ Take night flights and sleep
- ☐ Take short flights
- ☒ Listen to music
- ☒ Talk to other people
- ☐ Travel with friends
- ☐ Travel alone
- ☐ Read
- ☒ Watch a movie
- ☐ Play a game
- ☐ Do work from the office
- ☐ Eat
- ☐ Drink
- ☐ Move around
- ☒ Breathe deeply and relax
- ☐ Other. List: _____

_____

_____

20. Honestly, have you really tried to improve and become more comfortable flying?

- ☐ No
- ☒ Yes

Look over your results. What conclusion can you make about you and flying? Note especially:

- Your flying history
- What really bothers you about flying
- What you could do to make yourself comfortable when flying

Physical Symptoms

Tension created when confronting a fear can manifest itself in a number of different physical symptoms. Each symptom is a reaction to stress. The severity of the symptom may vary but the cause is still the same—tension. Many people get some preflight symptoms, some get in-flight symptoms, and a few people suffer after the flight is over.

Each of us experiences anxiety in his or her own way. Let's look at some of the more common anxiety-related physical complaints. If you believe your problem may be caused by some illness, or if it will make you more comfortable, consult your physician. Tension-produced physical symptoms will lessen as you learn to relax. These symptoms are normal physical reactions to stress. Relieve the stress and the symptoms will vanish.

Shortness of Breath

When very tense, many people find it difficult to take a full breath. The person who suffers from shortness of breath can even feel as if he is going to suffocate. Imagine how you would feel if you were suffocating—a first-class panic emergency situation if ever there was one.

Shortness of breath is caused by muscle tension around the chest. The muscles surrounding your chest can become very tight—much like the muscle tension many people feel in their shoulders. Even though you feel as if you cannot breathe, in reality you cannot *not* breathe. If you don't believe me, simply try not to breathe. After a couple of minutes, you will breathe—guaranteed. You see, breathing is controlled by your involuntary nervous system. That is why you breathe when asleep. And it is also why you cannot *not* breathe.

If you suffer from shortness of breath, what you are feeling is admittedly very alarming. It is not dangerous. Again, acceptance and relaxation are the proper prescriptions.

Hyperventilation

Hyperventilation is the opposite of shortness of breath. Hyperventilation means overbreathing, or rapid breathing. This type of fast breathing will lower the carbon dioxide level in your blood. The physical result of low carbon dioxide levels is a feeling of being light-headed, with tingling hands and feet. Again, your involuntary nervous system will ensure that you do no harm to yourself. You will get enough air to survive. Shortness of breath and rapid breathing indicate tension and stress. They do not mean you have a bad or weak heart.

As a nervous reaction, hyperventilation is quite common. Once you know and can accept what is happening, most of the problem is over. Usually just consciously slowing your breathing will be enough. If hyperventilation continues, cup your hand over your mouth or nose or use a handkerchief (no one will know what you are doing) and breathe into it. This type of breathing allows you to rebreathe your own breath, which in turn will increase the amount of carbon dioxide in your blood. Once the carbon dioxide level rises, your symptoms will pass. Hyperventilation is so common that airline companies train their crews to recognize and treat the problem. Again, it may be scary, but it is not dangerous.

Anxiety is directly related to breathing. All relaxation exercises include breathing exercises. Remember this: if you are anxious, you are not breathing correctly. If you are breathing correctly, you cannot be anxious.

Feeling Weak

Feeling weak is another rather common nervous complaint. When you feel weak, your body chemistry has changed. Let's learn what is happening to your body.

You supply energy to your body by burning glucose, a form of sugar. When you use your available supply of glucose, you are low on energy. You will feel weak and possibly cold. Being tense uses up a lot of energy. A normal body will produce all the glucose it needs. However, if you are very tense, you are burning glucose faster than your body is producing it. Using glucose faster than your body produces it will result in low blood sugar and low energy. Your body will resupply itself with glucose if you give it a chance. If you are tense and start to feel weak, give your body a few moments of rest or have a bite to eat. By the way, it is a good idea to eat a light meal an hour or so before you fly.

Poor breathing and the aftermath of a shot of adrenaline can also contribute to feeling weak and shaky. Some people hold their tension in their legs. If your legs stay tense for a long time, they will feel weak. However, even if you think your legs will not hold up—guess what? No matter how weak your legs may feel, even if they tremble, they will support you.

Just knowing what is happening physically is all the help many people need to overcome and find relief from nervous symptoms.

Muscle Tension

Every day millions of people experience muscle tension, which is almost always a sign of stress. From upset stomachs to tension headaches, tight muscles reign supreme as the number one symptom of stress.

What should you do when your muscles just tense up involuntarily?

The answer is movement. When we are startled, we momentarily stop, tensing muscles while adrenaline is pumped into our system. Whenever you notice yourself becoming tense, breathe deeply and move around. Don't just sit and think. When you are scared, physical movement will even lessen the feeling of fright. Staying rigid will prolong and agitate the condition.

Irregular Heartbeats

Under tension, your heart muscle may beat erratically. Your heart is adjusting to new conditions and stimuli. Often referred to as a missed heartbeat, what actually occurs is that your heart's timing is changing—it is getting faster or slower. Your heart might take two fast beats, pause, then beat unevenly for another beat or two. It will settle down. Do not scare yourself and add a second fear by saying something like, "I think I'm going to die if I don't get off this airplane."

Irregular heartbeats are common.

You do not panic if your car occasionally backfires or does not start on the first twist of the key. Well, your heart sometimes doesn't operate like a perfect Swiss watch. Many young and healthy people have occasionally irregular heartbeats called *extra systoles*. If your nerves are overly sensitized, you are probably prone to paying attention to unfamiliar body sensations such as irregular heartbeats. Preoccupation with body sensations just adds fuel to the fire. Remember, it will take some time for your body to readjust as your nerves quiet down.

Extra systoles can be brought on by alcohol, caffeine, nicotine, and fear. The treatment is to know what is happening and not make things worse. Lessen your intake of alcohol, caffeine, or nicotine, especially if you notice an abrupt physical change when using these chemicals. Moderate exercise will also help regulate heartbeats. Irregular or missed heartbeats do not mean you are going to have a heart attack.

Heart Palpitations

Because of nervous tension, a heart can develop bursts of quick heartbeats called *palpitations*. Physically you might get sweaty, feel hot, and have a tingling sensation in your extremities.

Your heart is a strong muscle and is not going to be damaged by rapid beating. Frequent rapid heartbeats do warrant a visit to your doctor. The American Heart Association advised me that a heart can beat at a rate of over 120 beats per minute (twice as fast as the normal heart rate) for months and suffer no damage.

Heart palpitations are a temporary upset in the timing of heartbeats—often started by a startling experience. It is important, as always, not to make matters worse by adding a second fear. If your attack occurs while at an airport or when flying, do not run and hide. Your heart will slow down as you relax.

If you continue to think about your heartbeat obsessively you are contributing to the problem. Let your heart beat away—fast, slow, or irregular. Once you have had a physical checkup, paying attention to your heart rate provides nothing but a useless concern.

Dizziness

Seeing the room weave back and forth and feeling dizzy and unsteady can be caused either by a biological imbalance or by nerves. Consult your physician. Severe vertigo is almost always caused by a chemical imbalance or other physical abnormality.

Mild dizziness is usually of nervous origin. Tension can restrict the blood flow to your brain and cause you to feel light-headed. As with most other nervous reactions, there is no real danger. Although some people fear this, I have never heard of a passenger who actually fell over because of nervous vertigo. Once you and your physician have ruled out organic causes, continue ahead with the proper attitude. Try not to obsess on your body sensations—accept and let the dizziness do its worst. You will be okay, and you will not pass out.

Vertigo can also be caused by changes in blood pressure, long periods of bending over, and standing up too quickly. Getting a little dizzy occasionally is normal and nothing to be concerned about.

Fear of Vomiting

Tension can cause some people to lose their appetite, others develop a craving to eat, and others feel nauseated. Fear that you might vomit is called emetophobia. It is easy to understand why this is an especially sensitive issue for some people aboard an airplane.

Understand that actual airsickness is very, very rare these days. If motion gives you a feeling of nausea, an over-the-counter motion-sickness pill should relieve your symptoms.

Nausea caused by nerves and tension can occur anytime. Aboard an airplane is admittedly a lousy place to feel nauseated. But no matter how nauseated you might feel, you will not ac-

71

tually vomit. Tension does cause nausea, but it takes much more than a case of nerves to actually make someone sick.

Sensitive Skin

Your skin is the largest organ of your body. Under stress, your skin will always be more sensitive. If you are extremely tense, a slight breeze can cause quite a personal disturbance. A change in room temperature, especially if it is too cool, can make an already tense person even more tense. Some people panic if they are too hot (thermophobia) while others have a difficult time tolerating the cold (frigophobia).

All airplanes are able to regulate the temperature inside the cabin. It is one of the flight engineer's jobs. Individual air vents and blankets provide ways for each passenger to have the exact temperature he or she prefers.

If tense, I recommend you keep warm because cold temperatures tend to make us tense our muscles even more. If you are warm, you will feel more relaxed.

Blushing is caused by a sudden release of blood to the skin's surface. Trying not to blush will only aggravate the condition. The less attention you can pay to blushing, the better. Blushing does not indicate repressed anger, sexual desires, or guilt. You might personally be embarrassed by blushing, but blushing is not dangerous. Blushing is a problem only if one thinks he should not blush.

Fainting

Remember the movie where the lady screams and faints at the sight of a mouse? Well, that's the movies. In reality, people do not actually faint as a nervous response. Feeling faint is not uncommon, but actually fainting is highly unlikely. The fear is the fear that you *might* faint—good old second fear again.

If you feel faint, rest a few minutes and then move along with as little concern about what happened as possible. You will be surprised at how beneficial the right attitude can be. As with other nervous symptoms, acceptance is very important.

Shock is different from feeling faint due to fear. Following a trauma, such as an automobile accident, one can suffer shock. Shock can cause you to pass out—nervous tension will not.

Shakes and Screams

For this last group of nervous symptoms, let's include trembling, cold hands, sweating palms, and the feeling that you are going to run up and down the aisle of the airplane screaming.

If you are concerned about your symptom, you are a victim of a body/mind con game. The con game works like this. You take a normal person and condition that person's nerves to a point where they are a bit oversensitive. Then add a little stress and wait for a physical symptom to show up. When some symptom shows up, the mind says, "Watch out! Something is wrong. Alert." The body reacts with more tension, and the mind responds, "Mayday, Mayday. Things are really getting bad now. Panic time." And the body responds with even more tension. More tension, more symptoms. More symptoms, more tension.

How do you win this body/mind con game? As you would any con game—don't play. If your mind yells, "Panic," and you respond with, "Ho hum," you win.

6
FEAR
RECOVERY

What situations or things trigger your fear-tension cycle? The questionnaire in the last chapter should have provided you with a good idea of what is happening when you push the panic button. Armed with this information, you can now get started and construct a personalized step-by-step plan to lessen your fear of flying.

To become more comfortable in the air, you definitely do not need to deal with each and every little thing that might bother you. You need to be concerned only with items that limit what you want to accomplish. If a postman is afraid of dogs or if a truck driver develops a fear of vehicles, then these fears limit their lives. If your fear of flying applies only to flying in small airplanes, then you can probably live without confronting this particular fear. It is commendable when someone overcomes a fear just because he wants to do it. It builds confidence. However, our concern here is not with conquering all fears. We are interested in deal-

75

ing only with a fear that inhibits or keeps you from flying.

Motivation

The first thing you need to do is to determine if you really want to lessen or rid yourself of your fear of flying.

Of course, all of us want to avoid suffering, and anxiety, tension, and panic are some of the world's most painful forms of suffering. I know that when panic strikes, it seems truly unbearable, and we will do almost anything to relieve the pain. It is accepted and understood that everyone is motivated to not hurt. My question still is, are you motivated enough to rid yourself of your fear? To change requires personal desire and motivation. If you do not want to or don't have to change, you won't. This is true for a fear of flying. If you aren't motivated, then it just isn't important enough for you to deal with your fear at this point in your life.

It is okay if you decide not to deal with your fear of flying. The choice is yours.

Which of the statements below seems to be closest to how you feel? Watch out for excuses and rationalizations, such as, "It's normal to be afraid of airplanes," or "I don't fly that often anyway." Take your time and be honest.

- At this time, I am not really interested in confronting my fear of flying.
- I would like to lessen my fear of flying; however, it is not a really important thing for me.

- I would like to lessen my fear of flying, but I am full of doubt and suspicion. I haven't tried because I am not sure I can do it.
- I would like to lessen my fear of flying. I have tried, but I don't think I can do it.
- It is really very important to me to rid myself of my fear of flying.

Look at your answer to determine your level of motivation.

It is easy to become discouraged or forget about your fears until you again come face-to-face with them. You need to be motivated to change. Remember, most fears are habits. What you learned, you can unlearn.

The Goal

To get somewhere, it is necessary to know where you are going. You will need a goal.

It will be necessary to prepare yourself to be in situations that are uncomfortable for you. Fortunately, this can and should be done progressively. You do not want to start out by terrorizing yourself.

The first goal will be to confront selected, relatively small fears. Next, you will want to confront increasingly scary circumstances. This is so you will build confidence and lessen the grip fear has on you.

Your final goal is a personal decision you must make about you and flying. Hopefully, all your fears about flying will quickly vanish and you will learn to love flying. Many onetime grounded aviophobics become hearty travelers. What level of success you desire is a personal decision you have to make. Some people will be satisfied with being able to get aboard a jet for a short flight, like it or not. Others will choose just to learn to reduce panic—they really do not desire to fly unless they absolutely have to. On the other hand, you may wish to learn to enjoy flying because it is necessary for your business. The choice is yours.

Only you can decide your goal and to what extent you are willing to invest yourself to obtain this goal.

Write a flying goal for yourself. Make your goal reasonable, specific, and obtainable. Here are some sample goals:

My goal is simply to go on my first airplane ride. I will select a short jet flight from Baltimore to Washington, D.C., round trip, thirty-five minutes each way.

My goal is to fly with my family from Seattle to Hawaii next summer.

My goal is to be able to fly with my husband. He is a private pilot, and small airplanes really terrify me. I want to be able to travel with my husband.

My goal is to be able to fly without either drinking my way onto the plane or taking tranquilizers.

My goal is to be able to actually enjoy the flights I take as part of my work. Usually I am tense before and during the flights. Flying adds a lot of unnecessary stress to my life.

What is your goal? Be reasonable. Don't set a goal you are not truly motivated to reach. Be honest with yourself.

The Plan

Now to obtain your flying goal, you will need a plan. There are three elements in forming a successful plan to become more comfortable flying.

- Plan your recovery step-by-step.
- Start with the easy fears first.
- Proceed at a moderate pace.

What you will be using is called a Progressive Recovery Plan.

The reason you want your plan to be step-by-step is so that you can gradually gain confidence. Starting with the easy fears first and going at a moderate pace will allow time for sensitized nerves to quit overreacting. Your body needs time to readjust. I know confronting a fear can be very difficult—at times even impossible. But I assure you—you can do it. Some days will be easier than others, and there will probably be setbacks. It takes a lot of courage to try, and you can be proud of yourself for having the courage to try.

Here are three examples of actual Progressive Recovery Plans. In each example, I would like you to notice the three key elements: step-by-step planning, starting with the easy fears first, and proceeding at a moderate pace. You cannot rush recovery. As a matter of fact, rushing or starting with too big a fear can cause additional stress and actually slow down the recovery process.

"My worst fear is being enclosed. The door on a plane shutting is by far the strongest panic cue for me. Also, the longer the flight, the more uptight I am.

"On the other hand, heights and turbulence present no problems for me. In fact, I like landings for they mean I am soon to be untrapped.

"My goal was to learn not to panic when enclosed and to be able to travel on non-stop flights of up to four hours. You see, I would always have a travel agent book me on flights that were an hour or less in duration. As you might imagine, I felt foolish. It was very inconvenient to take the short hops and my tickets usually cost me more. I was really motivated to change.

"My Progressive Recovery Plan consisted of taking longer and longer flights until I could travel for periods of four hours without experiencing any preflight or in-flight anxiety.

"I still don't like long flights. But I won't go out of my way to avoid them."

Sherry
Age 36

"My fear is getting on any plane. I shudder at the thought. I was on one flight as a child and still remember that I cried the whole way.

"It isn't easy for me to go to airports unless I am 100 percent sure I won't have to get on the plane—even for a moment.

"I wanted to be able to fly, not for work, but so I could enjoy life more and go places with my friends.

"My plan was to get on airplanes that weren't going anywhere. Through a Fear of Flight Clinic given at our local college, I was able to make arrangements, along with others, to board airplanes on the ground at the airport. It was really helpful to get familiar with the plane little by little. At first I needed a lot of reassurance just to get aboard the plane on the ground. After a few visits, I was ready for my next step—a short trip in a commuter-type plane. I selected the shortest flight available, fifteen minutes, and traveled with a good friend.

"My goal was to progressively take longer trips. Once I got over the initial fear, I learned to enjoy flying. I still get uncomfortable at the thought of flying but once on my way, I rarely have problems now."

Tony
Age 42

"I have never liked to fly. Turbulence and the thought of getting airsick are my fears. If the flight is even a little bumpy— it's a sure panic attack for me. I used to stare at the Fasten Seat Belt sign apprehensively, just waiting for it to light up.

"I need to fly for work. I hide my fear because I'm afraid of looking weak and maybe damaging my opportunities for promotion.

"My goal is to get over my attitude of impending doom. I normally took Dramamine and a few drinks before every flight, regardless of the time or circumstance. I was a walking zombie before I would get aboard any plane.

"My plan is to get over my fear of getting sick and learn to handle in-flight turbulence without tensing up. I started with visits to, of all things, amusement parks, following Ken's advice. Sure enough, the same old fear was there when I approached the roller coaster. I needed to start with the 'kiddy' rides. Once I worked my way up to the rides that turn upside down, I was eager to try my newfound courage in a plane.

"Turbulence on a plane was anticlimactic after mastering the amusement park rides. I learned that movement doesn't need to be scary, and I am not going to get airsick. Learning the causes of air turbulence also helped me become more comfortable."

Beth
Age 27

As you can see from these case examples, the formula for success in dealing with fear of flying is:

- Checking your motivation
- Identifying your fears
- Setting your personal flying goal
- Developing a Progressive Recovery Plan

Your Own Plan

Now it is time for you to develop your own personal Progressive Recovery Plan. To set up your plan, first review your goal. Next, select a starting point that deals with a relatively easy fear. What you want to do is design a tailor-made plan to reach your goal. Start easy and progressively confront more difficult fears, step-by-step, at a moderate pace.

Here is a sample Progressive Recovery Plan with a goal of flying to Hawaii. Look at how each step gets the person closer to her goal.

GOAL: Fly to Hawaii with my family

MAIN FEARS: Leaving home, airplane crashes, heights

STEP 1: Read a book about airline safety.

STEP 2: Go to the airport with my husband. Maybe have dinner there.

STEP 3: Go to the airport alone. Visit the observation tower and watch planes arriving and departing.

STEP 4: Find a travel agent. Explain my plan and select a short daytime flight that isn't crowded.

STEP 5: Go to a tall building downtown and practice looking from the top floor for at least thirty minutes.

STEP 6:   Buy an airline ticket for my
            "practice flight." Make ar-
            rangements for my husband
            and me to go—when I feel
            ready.

STEP 7:   Go on my practice flight with
            my husband.

STEP 8:   Select a different flight that is
            at least forty-five minutes long.
            Plan to travel one way in the
            day and return at night. Travel
            with my sister.

STEP 9:   Schedule our trip to Hawaii.
            Go one way in first class and
            return in coach class (if I don't
            need to travel in first class
            both ways to be comfortable). I
            will go on a wide-body plane
            and not sit next to the window.

STEP 10:   Maybe look out the window
            during the return flight if I feel
            ready to give it a try.

You may make as many progressive steps to
reach your goal as you feel you need. I have
found six to ten steps average and usually ad-
equate. Remember, step-by-step, easy to hard,
at a moderate pace.

Whether you have never flown or just want
to learn to be more comfortable flying, take your
first step only when you are ready. Don't rush
yourself or let others rush you. You will be experiencing what are fearful events for you. You

cannot expect to feel at ease, and your nerves will almost surely play tricks on you. Discouragement, differences in the way you feel inside, changes in attitudes, and frustration—these are the obstacles you will be facing.

When you put your plan into operation you will be placing yourself in fear-producing situations. It is unreasonable to expect that you will have 100 percent success right from the start. The important thing is to keep at it. The way to peace is by going through fear, not by going around fear. You cannot just tell yourself to stop worrying or in any other way avoid your fear if you wish to develop confidence and learn how to handle frightening situations.

Whatever you resist will persist.

We will cover putting your plan to work and handling setbacks in the next two chapters. But before we move on, let's look at some sample plans for dealing with common fears associated with flying—claustrophobia (fear of enclosed spaces) and agoraphobia (fear of traveling).

Claustrophobia: Fear of Enclosed Spaces

GOAL:	Go flying on a round-trip flight of over one hour
MAIN FEAR:	Being enclosed
STEP 1:	Go inside a small room in your home. Stay inside thirty minutes with the door shut, unlocked.
STEP 2:	Go inside the same small room. Stay inside thirty minutes with the door locked.

STEP 3: Go inside a small closet. Stay five minutes with the door shut and the light on.

STEP 4: Go inside a closet. Stay fifteen minutes with the door locked and a light on.

STEP 5: Go inside a closet. Stay thirty minutes with the door locked and the light off.

STEP 6: Take an elevator ride. Ride one floor in an uncrowded elevator.

STEP 7: Take an elevator ride. Ride at least ten floors.

STEP 8: Take an elevator ride. Ride at least ten floors. Pick a crowded elevator.

STEP 9: Take an uncrowded short (fifteen to thirty minutes) commuter flight.

STEP 10: Take a flight of at least one hour on a wide-body jet.

Agoraphobia: Fear of Traveling

GOAL: Go on my first flight

MAIN FEAR: Panic away from home

STEP 1: Go for a walk around your neighborhood. Go by yourself and visit some new streets and places.

STEP 2: Go to and stay in a crowded store near your home for at least thirty minutes by yourself.

STEP 3: Go to a place not too far from your home that you've been avoiding. Stay there at least fifteen minutes.

STEP 4:   Take a taxi or bus ride for thirty minutes away from home. Go by yourself or with a friend. (If you are with a friend, don't hide your fear. Explain why you are taking the trip.)

STEP 5:   Take a train or bus ride to a place one hour away.

STEP 6:   Go to a crowded shopping center. Stay at least two hours. Have something to eat or drink.

STEP 7:   Go to an airport during a busy time. Visit the observation deck and watch planes come and go. Imagine you are on a departing plane.

STEP 8:   Buy a ticket on a short, uncrowded flight. Go on the flight with a friend. Return the same day.

STEP 9:   Go on a plane ride to the same destination as before. This time stay overnight.

STEP 10:   Take a plane trip, by yourself, to a place you have never been before. Stay at least one night. Don't shelter yourself on this trip. Go to a movie, shopping, or to a restaurant.

Now you know what you need to do—let's learn how to do it.

7

GETTING YOUR PROGRAM TO WORK

Designing a reasonable and obtainable Progressive Recovery Plan will not cure you of your fear unless you put your plan to work. To recover you will need to learn how to face your fears successfully. And no matter what else you do, and no matter what others may tell you, the way to cure a fear is by facing it. You may be saying to yourself, "Is he really saying that the only way to cure or lessen my fear of flying is to go flying?" Yes, that's it. But, it is not at all a case of grin and bear it. You definitely do not need to force yourself onto a plane. The way to recovery is progressive. The key is the way in which you learn to handle your fears.

The way in which each of us reacts to fear is learned. It is a habit. Some people shake, some sweat, some talk loud, and others clam up. Let's learn a new way of reacting to fear.

From now on, each time you face a fearful situation, you will want to:

- Confront your fear
- Communicate your experience

• Continue—don't run and hide

> "Once the phobic recognizes that a phobic attack is a process—something they control and can do something about—they are on their way to recovering."

Dr. Manuel Scain
Psychiatrist
White Plains (New York) Phobia Clinic

> "I think the largest obstacle to the recovery of phobias is the attitude of the phobic. Most sufferers are ashamed of their illness. Once they discover that they are not alone, that they are not some freak—this is very helpful to the recovery process."

Dr. Arthur Hardey
Menlo Park, California
On *60 Minutes*, CBS

Confronting Your Fears

What you need to do is directly experience your fear. It is a case of looking right into the eye of the tiger. Using drugs, thinking about something else, avoiding fearful things, making up reasons why you should be afraid—these are all ways of not confronting your fears directly.

Confronting your fears may sound terrible. A client once told me, "If I could confront my fears then I wouldn't be asking you to help me. You're telling me to do exactly what I cannot do." First, realize that you will be confronting easy fears. I am not asking you to slay a dragon or fly around the world. I am suggesting dinner at the airport. Second, the way you confront your fears can and should be under your conscious control. You can learn how to handle fear successfully. If you are preoccupied with thinking about fear and trying to figure out how not to experience fear, you are creating a lot of unnecessary stress and tension.

Once you learn how to change the way you react to fear you will probably surprise yourself. Most people say "It's not nearly as bad as I thought it would be." Learning to face fear can help you deal better with other areas of your life.

"My name is Betty. I am thirty-five years old. I have been afraid to fly—afraid of anything more than a foot above the ground—ever since childhood. It took me a broken marriage and a ruined self-image before I was willing to confront my fear of flying. After learning how fear worked and that I could control my physical symptoms, especially feeling faint, I was able to gradually test myself by going up elevators and then to high-rise buildings. After mastering my fear of heights, it was easy for me to let go of my fear of flying. The fascinating thing is that when I learned not to fear heights and flying, I also learned how to face other fears. My self-image has improved. I feel good about myself."

Let me add a personal example about the advantages of confronting your fears. Many years ago when I was first taking flying lessons, I feared clouds. Those friendly, puffy white clouds looked like demons to me. I was afraid of what might happen if I flew into one. Maybe it would be very turbulent, and I would get sick or get vertigo and be unable to control the airplane. Maybe I would panic when I couldn't see the ground. What if I got lost or the airplane turned upside down? You see, I had invented some fears you probably have never even thought of. I just would not fly if there were clouds in the sky. I was forced to cancel training sessions and pay for airplanes I never used—all because of a fear I would not confront.

Communicate

Embarrassed, I finally told a friend about my fear. Admittedly, I tried to sound as if clouds really could be dangerous (which they aren't). Once I talked about my fear and quit hiding it, I immediately started to feel better about myself. Soon thereafter, I set up a progressive plan with my flight instructor to venture into the clouds. We started with little clouds for a few minutes, then extended the amount of time we flew in clouds. Next, and when I felt ready, we ventured into larger clouds, slowly extending the duration of our flights.

Well, as you might have guessed, my fear of what might happen was much different from what did happen. By communicating my fear, I was able to see what I was doing. Talking can do wonders. And with the use of a gradual, progressive plan, I was able to safely test my concerns and learn not to be afraid of clouds.

Communication equals movement. You are stuck with those fears that you are unwilling to communicate.

Understand this: by communicate, I do not mean sitting around verbally trying to justify, defend, or make excuses for your fear. True communication means being willing to tell things just as they are. If you are embarrassed to go flying because flying makes your hands tremble, then the truth is that flying makes your hands tremble. That's the way it is for you now. Don't lie about it or hide it.

Remember, your symptoms are normal—just exaggerated. You are not sick, your nerves are just very sensitive. So what? Being afraid doesn't make you less of a person.

> "We understand that, unfortunately, there are a sizable number of people who are apprehensive about flying. I would strongly suggest that a fearful flyer let us know of their concerns. Our crews are trained to help uncomfortable passengers. An apprehensive passenger is much better off to not hide and be ashamed of their fear."
>
> Stan Brown
> Vice President, Sales
> Eastern Airlines

Continue

Back to my example about my fear of flying in the clouds. If after one trip into the clouds I had said, "Well, that's that," and never again confronted my fear, I would most likely still be grounded on all but sunny days. It is necessary to continue. You need to be tenacious and not give up. Habits die slowly. If you are going to succeed at quitting smoking, you can't just skip one cigarette and say, "This is too hard to do." You must continue. Most people who quit smoking started and failed many times. They knew what they wanted and stuck to it.

Confront, communicate, and continue. Believe me, I know how very difficult this can be. You will get discouraged at times. Success requires perseverance. But, it does work and you can cure yourself.

You also need to recognize that dealing with your fears is a very personal matter. Other people can empathize with you, but they can't feel what you feel. Only you know how big a battle you are facing. The battle is inside and it takes real courage to face your fears. You can be proud of yourself regardless of what others may think or say.

Types of Fears

It is essential that you recognize your own responses when you come face-to-face with a fear. When you can recognize when and how you react, you are well on your way to recovery.

For example, suppose you get aboard a flight anticipating an uncrowded plane and discover you must sit between two people you do not know. This change could make anyone uncomfortable. You start to experience a feeling of being hemmed in—trapped. This feeling of being trapped is a first fear. How you handle this initial experience of fear is very important. You need to recognize the first signs of fear and not add a second fear.

If you say to yourself, "I have to get out of here. I can't take this," with each word you say, you are adding tension and increasing the likelihood of a panic attack. You are adding a second fear. You might say to yourself, "What if I get sick or the airplane door sticks and I am stuck here?" More second fear—more tension—more panic. A person experiencing severe anxiety does not think clearly and may easily become confused and disoriented.

On airplanes, where one is exposed to the public in an enclosed space with literally no way out—well, the problem is obvious. The solution begins with identifying the difference between first fear and second fear. It is not the fear itself that is the problem. The problem is the way you handle your fear.

The real fear is a fear of what will happen if you panic. The phobic person is scared of being scared. You must learn that it is okay to be scared and that you will be all right. You must learn not to fear the experience of fear.

Reducing Panic

How do you cope with feelings of panic, especially when the panic strikes fast and there is no escape? You cope by learning not to react to panic. Once you learn to accept changes in feelings, body sensations, and thoughts, you will improve. Panic feeds on panic. Once you stop adding second fears and let panic do its worst, you have stopped the panic reaction.

No matter how scared you are of flying, if you can recognize when fear begins and not add a second fear, you will become more comfortable flying. Guaranteed. If you do not run from panic, you will succeed.

Talking to Yourself

If you think you cannot stand the panic feeling—join the band. Being terrified is terrifying to everybody. You may think it is especially bad for you—but so does everybody. If you think this program is too much to ask of you, if you think that I don't know how much you suffer or how hard you have already tried to get better, you're wrong—I know and I understand.

You tell yourself you are too weak or your panic is worse than most. This mental conversation with yourself is more second fear. This type of talking to yourself adds to the problem. Recognize this and stop adding to the problem. I know you suffer, and I also know that at times you may think you will never get better. Give yourself

some credit—you can do it. If you can't think
something positive about yourself or flying, then
talking less to yourself is a good prescription. You
will be pleasantly surprised of how much better
you will feel once you stop talking negatively to
yourself.

Acceptance

Even when you recognize when and how you
add second fear, even when you stop adding to
the problem, recovery is going to take time.
Habits just simply take time to change. There
is no instant cure. During the time when your
body is readusting, getting stronger, and your
nerves are becoming less and less sensitive
you may still feel some anxiety. But each day
you will get better.

To confront and accept your nervous symptoms is a very important part of the recovery.
As a matter of fact, when you can accept your
nervous symptoms and not add second fear by
brooding over or exaggerating them, recovery
is imminent.

Changing

As you work your way progressively toward
your goal, strange new feelings may arise. This
is a normal part of change. For years you have
conditioned yourself against feeling fear. Now
you are choosing to confront your fears. It is

understandable that you may react strongly. It is as if your body were saying, "Hey, what's going on here? I am accustomed to running away and hiding from fear, not confronting it."

It is normal for your body to feel strange when you begin to confront things that you have been avoiding for years. When you start your Progressive Recovery Plan, be prepared for new feelings and thoughts.

There is no rush, take your time, but do not give up.

If you are not ready for a flight on the particular day you are scheduled to fly—reschedule. Some days you will be stronger than others. Don't let yourself get discouraged and give up. Don't tell yourself, "I'll never get better." You will get better. Confront, communicate, and continue, continue, continue.

I once got together with a friend to fly to Palm Springs, California, for a short vacation. This trip would be his first flight and he was scared. He felt apprehension, not sure if he was ready to go. In the process of checking baggage and getting our tickets, my friend added a lot of second fear. By the time we were ready to depart, he was a wreck. We boarded, and *wham*—panic. My friend dashed off the airplane. This is another critical time. Does he face the rest of the day with defeat, embarrassment, and apologies? Does he add discouragement and be hard on himself? No. A better attitude is just to say, "Oh, well, that didn't work." A little humor helps a lot. Then it's off for a nice meal and an alternate plan—like driving or trying again tomorrow.

Patience and Acceptance

It is understandable to want to get over your fears quickly. Some people are naturally more aggressive. They like to roll up their sleeves and tackle a problem head-on. Well, when it comes to learning new ways of handling fear, this superman attitude is likely to worsen the problem. Patience and acceptance are much more valuable traits.

The compulsive, high-achieving type of personality often creates huge amounts of internal tension. This type of person will usually have a very difficult time accepting fear as a normal part of life. He will try to power through any fearful situation. Generally speaking, if you have a need to control and are an aggressive person, a little repair on your overall attitude will be necessary before you will be able to lessen your fear-tension cycle. It is also a good prescription for living longer.

If you can accept the frustration, the changes in feelings, the strange thoughts, if you can accept and do not add to whatever may happen, you will become stronger. With acceptance, you fears will become more manageable and your nerves will settle down. Remember, your symptoms are nothing but exaggerated reactions to tension. They are not dangerous and, even though you may think so, they are also not unique.

The key is to accept what is and not make things worse. Confront, communicate, and continue.

Attitude

Once you have control over your nervous reactions, flying comfortably is largely the establishment of the right attitude. You have changed your attitudes.

If you switch from an attitude of fear to an attitude of "Sometimes I get uptight flying," you have come a long way toward recovery. Start right now.

- Drop the word *phobia* altogether.
- Quit thinking of flying as a big negative in your life.
- Stop dwelling on your failures.
- Start thinking about your successes.

You have to quit the "I can't" attitude and learn to be positive. You have the courage to do it. I am sure you are big enough to say, "Now I see what I have been doing wrong. I have been approaching flying in the wrong way. From now on, I will be more realistic about flying. It just isn't worth ruining my life because I wasn't born to love zipping along above the clouds."

With this attitude, you can't lose. With this attitude, you will build your self-esteem and capture the respect of others.

Flying Comfortably

Flying comfortably means different things to different people. While one person may think flying should be peaceful and relaxing, another person might experience flying as exciting, or boring, or tiring. Any of these beliefs about flying are fine. As long as you are satisfied with the way you fly, this is what matters.

For a person who has problems with flying, a large portion of the problem might be:

- His expectations about flying are unrealistic.
- He thinks he should never feel at all uncomfortable about flying.
- He thinks a nervous reaction is a sign of illness and a serious problem.

Let's clear this up right now. To be a normal, healthy passenger does not mean you will never become nervous when flying. Some flights may be lovely, smooth, and you will think, "This is what flying should be and I love it." Another flight is crowded, you are tired and in a bad mood. During this flight you experience a churning stomach and a strong desire to get off the airplane. This too is normal. There is absolutely nothing wrong with you. I know many stewardesses, pilots, and others who frequently travel by air and who sometimes hate the thought of flying. Life has its ups and downs. So does flying.

Important Reminders

- Some days will be easier than others. That's just the way it is.
- Thoughts and feelings may become strange. This is a normal part of recovery.

- Just because you are scared now doesn't mean you will always be scared. Fears come and fears go.

- With each success you become stronger. Let your feelings come. Don't resist.

- You cannot force recovery. Fighting yourself only makes things worse.

- Do not rush. Take your first step only when you are ready.

- Recovery lies in being able to "be with" your fears and not in running away from them.

- No matter how frightened you feel, you will be okay. The feeling will pass.

- Give fear time to pass. Don't add frightening thoughts. Make yourself as comfortable as you can until your fear passes.

- Don't become preoccupied with your physical symptoms. Get outside yourself and pay attention to other things.

- The first attack of panic is the worst. It gets easier. It physiologically cannot get worse.

- Successful people and unsuccessful people both experience fear. The difference is, some live with it, and some live to avoid it.

- You may never completely lose your fear of flying. But you *can* learn to cope effectively.

8
ACTIVE
RELAXATION

The radio announces a special discount fare to London. The television shows a happy husband and wife about to take off for their second honeymoon. Magazine articles show pictures of new, larger seats and elegant in-flight cuisine. The office hums with your co-workers' adventurous plans to fly here and there visiting relatives or off to some exotic island for the vacation of a lifetime. And there you are—stuck, embarrassed, and feeling unable to participate.

I can truly sympathize with you. Being unable to join in—in a sense disabled—is a lonely and discouraging feeling. The most unfortunate part is that the wall between you and freedom is more imaginary than real. By imaginary I do not mean your suffering isn't real. It is very real, and can be very painful. What I am saying is that the wall is mostly imaginary. If you can muster up enough strength to test that wall, I think you will find it is not as tall and confining as it seems.

If you are about ready to test yourself, you might find extra strength by simply getting fed up and angry at your fears. If you can become irritated at your fear of flying, it is a good sign you are ready for a change.

Controlling Tension

If you weren't tense, you wouldn't be scared. Remember, it just is not possible to be relaxed and scared at the same time. If you can relax, then goodbye fear. When it comes to flying, there are four times when people become tense—before the flight, during takeoff, en route, and upon landing.

To relax in the face of fear is a challenging task. You will not need to spend hours practicing relaxation (not that some time spent relaxing isn't a good prescription for most of us). What you will need to do is deliberately relax at a specific time. It is not so much a matter of relaxing—it's more a matter of not getting tense. But in case you should get tense, you will want to let go of any tension and return your muscles to a relaxed state as quickly as possible.

What you want to do is learn to relax on command. That means that if I say go, you should be able to relax in no more than two minutes. It is really quite simple and easy to do. This approach is called *active relaxation*.

Active Relaxation

Active relaxation differs from other forms of relaxation because the goal is not to train ourselves to be more relaxed persons overall. We want to attack tension quickly and on command. Another difference between active relaxation and other relaxation techniques is speed. To attain quick results, we will use movement to help us relax. Movement is one of the most effective techniques available to change tension into relaxation.

Aboard a flight you are instructed to sit down and fasten your seat belt. As you sit, not moving a muscle, you are doing exactly the opposite of what needs to be done.

Preflight Tension

To deal with preflight tension the main rule is not to allow yourself to become preoccupied with what is in the future. What you need to do is recognize when you are becoming preoccupied and what you are saying to yourself about your upcoming flight. If you work yourself into a tense state prior to your flight, it will make relaxing on the airplane that much more difficult.

Each time you catch yourself thinking about your upcoming flight, use what psychologists call *thought stoppage*. Thought stoppage is a very effective method for people who tend to think negatively (second fear) or think excessively about the future.

Use thought stoppage as soon as you notice

yourself thinking about your upcoming flight. Tell yourself to stop and take a deep breath, and then resume whatever you were doing. Do not let the thoughts continue. Every time you notice yourself thinking about your upcoming flight, use thought stoppage. You will notice that your negative thoughts will occur less frequently. Remember, do not dwell upon your upcoming flight. You can also help yourself by getting involved in an activity. For people who have a lot of preflight anxiety, I recommend they fly in the morning. There is no reason to waste a whole day constantly dealing with unwanted thoughts.

Use thought stoppage if you notice that you're thinking negative thoughts (second fear) such as "I'll never get over my fear of flying. I am probably near a nervous breakdown," or "If I get sick on board, what will I do? What will other people think of me?"

Each time you stop thinking negatively, you're being good to yourself. You will be pleasantly surprised at the results. If you notice that you are reluctant to change your thinking, reexamine your motivation. Do you really want to get over your fear?

You see, some people actually enjoy negative thinking. "The plane could be hijacked, the crew killed, and I would be forced to fly the airplane myself." A heroic thought but lousy conditioning.

Hopefully, you've also isolated what really bothers you the most and are being easy on yourself. If the length of the flight is what gives you the most problem, take shorter flights. If height is what causes you to be tense, sit in an aisle seat. If you know what bothers you, there is no reason to make yourself any more anxious than necessary. Avoid whatever fears are not necessary to confront. Remember your goal.

Takeoff Tension

If taking off is the worst part of flying for you, then your problem is to reduce tension during takeoffs, and to let go of tension after the flight is en route.

Regardless of what usually causes you to become tense, always try to stop tension before it builds up. The nip-it-in-the-bud approach is always going to be easier than seeking relief during a full-scale anxiety attack.

Back to handling takeoff tension. Now is a good time to use active relaxation.

After boarding the plane and being seated, close your eyes and take a complete breath. Inhale slowly and exhale slowly while counting from one to ten. Count slowly—don't rush. As you count, relax your legs, then your stomach— keep counting slowly—relax your chest, your shoulders, your arms, your neck, and finally your face. After counting to ten, take another complete breath. Simple, isn't it?

Now I want you to reach up and stretch, one arm at a time or both together. Next, while seated, reach down and touch your feet. Finally, move your head around from side to side or in a circular motion. Continue to take slow, full breaths. That's it. It's easy and it's effective.

By breathing fully, relaxing your muscles, and moving you will have reversed your fear-tension cycle. It takes about two minutes.

If, as the airplane begins its takeoff roll, you feel yourself tensing up, then without hurry:

- Take a full breath.
- Count from one to ten while . . .
- Relaxing feet to face.
- Take another full breath (don't rush it).
- Perform the movements—stretch, bend, and rotate your head.

I think you will discover that just having a plan—something specific you can do when you are tense—will provide you with a lot of security. Active relaxation will be more beneficial the more you use it. Don't hurry—it takes only a couple of minutes anyway. Be sure to do each part completely. Really breathe, let those muscles go limp, and use complete movements. Stretch—don't just raise your hand—really give yourself a good stretch. Remember, you're doing yourself a favor.

After the airplane has departed, your task is to stay relaxed. If taking off is the scariest part of flying for you, then once you're off the ground, it's time to enjoy the flight. There is only one takeoff per flight. The worst has passed.

In-Flight Tension

To relieve in-flight tension, once the airplane has taken off and the captain turns off the No Smoking sign, it is time for you to start using active relaxation. While sitting, take a full breath, count from one to ten, relax your muscles, breathe again, stretch, touch your toes, move your head from side to side. Once the captain has turned off the Fasten Seat Belt sign, actually get up and walk down the aisle of the airplane. If you are aboard a wide-body flight (and I recommend a wide-body if you haven't tried flying on one), go for a stroll around the airplane. Maybe get a magazine or visit the "blue room" (aviation language for "toilet"). The important and essential point is to practice movement and breathing. Do not let yourself become rigid.

Use these movements at least once per hour on longer flights. Believe me, the captain and the crew get up and move about—so should you. Just sitting at a desk for an hour or more can leave you stiff. Movement equals relaxation.

Landing Tension

As we have learned, airline pilots are very experienced. Many captains have logged an incredible hundred thousand–plus landings. Landings are safe.

But that doesn't mean you feel safe, does it? If landings make you tense, then that's just the way it is—for now anyway.

When do you start to get tense about landings? If you start thinking about landing long before the airplane begins its descent, then thought stoppage should be used. Do not let your thoughts run wild and intimidate you. You can control your thinking.

If you begin to tense up just prior to landing, then use the active relaxation techniques when you first notice any tension. A good time to start relaxing is when you hear the cabin crew announce, "Ladies and gentlemen, in preparation for landing, please put your tray tables and seats backs in their upright positions." With landing fear, you do not need to be concerned with tension lingering around. Once back on the ground, any residual tension is usually burned up looking for your bags, seeing friends, or finding transportation to your destination.

Minimizing Tensions

Active relaxation and thought stoppage are both excellent methods and will produce positive results. But why not make flying as easy as possible? I have been amazed how often someone who is afraid to fly seems to go out of his way to get the worst possible flight under the worst possible circumstances.

I recall one thirty-three-year-old female with a mild fear of flying. She didn't get too tense when flying. She really just hated heights. The last time she visited my office, she was a nervous wreck. She told me she had had a relapse. Her nerves were worse than ever, and now she thought that flying was scarier than it had ever been. I asked her about her last flight.

As she told me about her last flight, the reason for her increased tension and fear became clear. First, she went flying in a small plane (extra tension #1) piloted by a fellow she had been dating only two weeks and did not know very well (extra tension #2). The flight was at night (extra tension #3). Her date had only recently received his pilot's license (extra tension #4). The flight was turbulent (extra tension #5). To top it all off, she was just recovering from a head cold (extra tension #6), and hadn't told her date of her fear of heights and flying (extra tension #7).

It is easy to understand how these circumstances could leave one even more nervous.

When you fly, be nice to yourself. Avoid whatever stresses you can. If you do not like crowds, don't take a crowded plane. Once you have identified those things that bother you, there is absolutely nothing wrong with avoiding stress, as long as you still reach your goal.

Do not make things harder than they need to be. Get plenty of rest before you fly. And eat a light meal before you leave. Flying rested and with something in your stomach will help you effectively deal with any anxiety or any hassles that might pop up. During the flight, eat light and drink plenty of fluids. Wear loose, comfortable clothing. If you prefer to travel alone, then do so. You can meet up with your friends later. They will understand and accept the situation if you talk openly and honestly about your fears and your needs. And, of course, don't fly if you are feeling ill.

Diversions

It is a good idea to take aboard "goodies" to help pass the time. If you enjoy backgammon, bring your set with you. Those little electronic games can fill hours. If you enjoy reading, bring along a library if you wish. Sew, design a new house, arrange a party, or write letters to friends. Whatever you enjoy that doesn't create tension is a good idea to take with you when you fly.

Rewards

How about rewarding yourself for challenging the wild blue yonder? Good idea. If you like banana splits, how about promising yourself one the moment you land? Or maybe arrange a room for yourself in the best hotel in town. The idea is to give yourself as much incentive as possible to fly.

If your husband or wife is reluctant to travel by air, don't try to intimidate him or her into flying. If and when the courage is mustered—and it is true courage to face a fear—a reward and some congratulations at the end of the flight is a marvelous idea.

Booze and Pills

Many people take an assortment of chemicals to help them before and during a flight. The bars and lounges at airports always seem to be full. If you like to drink, I see no reason why you shouldn't. Of course, be reasonable, and never mix pills and booze. Airlines have a limit on the number of drinks you are allowed during a flight. You will not be served on board if you have had too much, and it is against the law to board an airplane in an intoxicated condition. If you get drunk, you might just find yourself waving goodbye to your flight. Drugs, tranquilizers, sleeping pills, and motion-sickness pills diminish external perceptions and can help ease the fear and reduce tension.

If tranquilizers provide you with relief, then take them if you feel you must. You won't get over your fears this way. Still, at times drugs can be a real benefit. It depends on the circumstances.

Understand that tranquilizers will not stop panic attacks. During a panic attack, the adrenaline that is shot into your system is too powerful a drug and works much faster than any tranquilizer or sleeping pill. Relaxation and acceptance are far more effective than drugs when and if panic strikes.

Just carrying drugs along "in case of an emergency" provides all the security some people need to get into the air. Learning to quiet down your fear and learning to relax are better prescriptions in the long run. But, if taking a trunkful of plastic dolls, a bushel of pills, a pillow, and your favorite stuffed teddy bear helps you participate in the world, you get my vote and support.

Do what you must to get yourself airborne. Just get on that plane.

9
HOW TO HANDLE SETBACKS

In the process of progressively training yourself to be more comfortable flying, you will likely experience some setbacks. You must remember that sensitized nerves and your habitual ways of reacting to fear are going to take time to change.

When you avoid adding second fear, you will become stronger almost immediately. With each success, you will gain increased confidence—and more confidence is exactly what you need.

It is important not to let a setback ruin your confidence. A setback is discouraging—so be discouraged. That is normal. But do not let temporary setbacks completely destroy you psychologically.

Panic attacks will come and go. Maybe you've successfully worked your way from a visit to the airport all the way to a cross-country flight. You feel cured. Then one day you are off to the airport for a relatively easy trip. With confidence, you board the airplane, have a seat, and *whamo*—a full dose of panic. You make some flimsy excuse and dash off the airplane.

You are discouraged and wonder if you will ever get better: "Must I always fear having another attack?" or "I will never be able to trust myself." Don't give up. What you experienced is a normal part of getting better.

Remember: confront, communicate, and continue—and continue means not giving up. So as soon as you are rested and ready, get back on that airplane.

It is common to add a second fear when a setback occurs: "Will I ever get better?" How about thinking: "Setbacks are a normal part of recovery. But I will not give up or make a big deal out of one isolated failure." Now *that* is a winning attitude.

What Causes Setbacks?

Here are the common conditions that will contribute to or cause a setback:

Worry

Stress is probably the most common cause of setbacks. When you are under stress, you won't be thinking as well as usual, and physical symptoms will be more common and will often be exaggerated.

Not Enough Rest

Not getting the proper amount of exercise or rest contributes to stress. If you are overtired, you are going to be emotionally and physically less tolerant than normal. Being overtired will increase the likelihood of a panic attack and a setback.

Poor Eating

If you have ever been on a diet, have you noticed that you are more irritable? That is normal—eating affects our emotionality. If you drink too much alcohol—well, I think we all know that someone with a hangover is not doing his best.

Forgetting What You Learned

Sometimes we simply forget to do what we know works. It is the same as learning to stretch before you run. One day, for no reason, you do not stretch. You end up with a pulled muscle and cuss at yourself for being so stupid. "I knew better." It happens. We all can laugh at ourselves on occasion.

Illness

Being sick is physically and psychologically stressful. If you have the flu, a cold, or any other physical illness, you are under stress. When you feel poorly, you are less capable of dealing effectively with additional stress—such as flying. If you are not feeling up to par, you probably should change your flight to a later date.

You May Be Undependable

If you are phobic about flying, one day you may feel ready and willing to go and the next day be absolutely terrified. It makes no sense. You are courageously struggling toward freedom. Yours is an internal, private struggle. People will try to understand, but they really cannot. No one can know what it is like unless he has personally experienced the fears, the panic, the mental confusion, or the helplessness a phobic person lives with.

A panic attack can strike rapidly and seemingly without warning. You may, in good faith, make plans to fly one day and need to cancel your reservation the next. Maybe you again feel strong and make your reservation, only to cancel at the last moment. You cannot expect people not to be frustrated with your undependable behavior. All you can do is tell the truth about your dilemma. Let your travel companions know of your potential undependability. I often recommend that the aviophobic arrange their travel plans so that, should reservations be made, broken and made again, other people's plans aren't ruined. If someone is relying on you to take a certain flight and an entire vacation will be ruined if you do not go, that is just more added stress. And the added stress will make it more likely you will have an attack and cannot go.

Some people find that traveling on impulse helps them gain confidence. If you have the money and time and feel ready, go! Every success breeds success.

Permission to Fail

Give yourself permission to fail. One hundred percent success should not be your goal because one hundred percent success isn't reasonable. You need to accept setbacks and disappointments. Setbacks are a normal part of recovery. Your mind will play tricks on you. Don't fret over failures or memories of past pain. Thoughts are thoughts—they are not reality. A good attitude is "I still think scary things about flying at times. So what! They are only thoughts. In reality, I am getting better and stronger each day."

You Think . . .

You think you are too old to recover. You think you are a coward. You think you can't do it. You think no one knows how much you suffer. You think you are mentally ill. You think you cannot trust yourself. You think you must have medication. You think yours is a special case. You think you are just not strong enough to change. You think you never can face your fears.

Welcome to the human race. You're normal.

What you *think* is not what counts. What you *do* is what really matters. Think what you will, just keep going forward.

Waiting

When traveling by air, there is a lot of waiting. Waiting is often the most difficult part of a trip. Waiting is tough. When waiting, it is all too easy to start thinking negatively about your upcoming flight.

You know what I mean. If you are going to the dentist at 10:00 A.M., that tends to make for a lousy breakfast. That is just the way it goes. Anticipating is a part of life, so don't let it become a bigger problem than it already is. Once you have managed to wait for the flight, you've made it through the roughest part. Make good use of thought stoppage and active relaxation while you are waiting.

Thinking Differently

Under stress you will have a tendency to question everything. "Why is the plane so late?" "Why does it take so long to fly there?" Often masking hostility, questions cause added stress and are often second fear. The underlying question may be "Why do I have to feel this bad?"

Thoughts can get crazy. "If the plane lands in the water and sinks, I can't swim." "Who will take care of my dog if I die?" "If the plane crashes into a mountain, they will never find my body." And on and on. Stop what thoughts you can, and do not dwell on the ones that keep hanging around, no matter how crazy and scary they might be.

Preoccupation with yourself and coping with a fearful event can leave you with a poor recall of events. If you forget a few things, so what? Keep sight of your goals. You will not forget anything really important. A lost bag or missed appointment is a small price to pay for personal success.

Mentally exhausted, often frustrated, sometimes discouraged, it is easy to see how you could lose your confidence. Confidence is a by-product of success. If you continue to progress, you will eventually succeed and confidence will grow. Recall what it was like learning some other new thing. For example, you were not confident when you first started riding a bike. Now that you can ride a bike, you are confident, right? You don't need confidence to start. You get confidence when you finish.

When tired and under stress, decisions, even small decisions, may seem impossible. Even deciding what you will have for lunch may be too much. I have written Chapter Ten, "Before You Fly," so that you can keep on track when flying. As with a poor memory, a few poor decisions are a small price for success.

Just slow down, take it one step at a time, and stay true to yourself and your goals.

When Friends Give Advice

Friends, relatives, your spouse, or even perhaps your pastor will, with good intentions, give you advice. You will probably hear:

- "Don't let it bother you."
- "You think you got problems. Listen to this . . ."
- "You'll get over it."
- "All you need to do is fly a few times and you will be okay."
- "I used to be scared. Look at me now. (Brag, brag.)"
- "Did your mother fear planes?"
- "It's just fear of heights."
- "You'll grow out of it."
- "I don't want to discuss it."
- "It's your problem."
- "If you don't want to be scared, you won't be."
- "You're responsible for your behavior. Choose not to be scared and you won't."
- "Trust in God. He will take care of you."
- "Take the train."

. And on and on. Don't get into an argument. Let others think what they may. You know what you need to do.

Psychological Games

There are many psychological games a person can play to avoid confronting fear. Be careful not to fall into one of these traps.

Help Me

This game consists of someone trying to get someone else to do what he must do for himself. "I'm so scared of flying, you must hold my hand." "I can't do it without you." As the famous psychiatrist Dr. Fritz Perls said, "We must all do our own dirty work."

You may ask for assistance, but do not play helpless.

Defender

"My fear is understandable because as a small child, my mother took me on an airplane, and it almost crashed." In this game, the person is obviously defending his fear. Don't rationalize fear. Defending your fear just makes fear stronger and more difficult to eliminate.

Catastrophizer

This is the game in which you build up your fears to be much worse than they actually are. You create a catastrophe. "There are more airplanes these days so there is more chance of having a midair collision." "Airline crashes are always fatal." Don't think negatively.

Silent Sufferer

In this game, the player just won't admit his fear. Admitting you are afraid is a necessary part of the recovery process. The silent sufferer is trying to look good and is embarrassed by anything he believes others may see as a fault or blemish.

Weakling

"I've never been very strong." "It's much too scary for me. I could never face flying." There is a big difference between imaginary weakness and a real limitation. Playing weak will keep you weak.

Rationalizer

Here the person justifies his fear. The player goes about telling how reasonable and justifiable his fear is. "Flying really is dangerous." "I'm not going to put my life in the hands of some jet jockey." "I've got a wife and kids." "I can't take the chance."

Doomed Victim

The doomed victim is probably the most frustrating of all psychological game players. He says, "I'm afraid to fly and there is nothing I can do about it." If you believe you can't, you can't.

In life you get either success or excuses. Let's succeed and not get caught in some psychological excuse game.

Professional Help

If you think you would like to consult with a professional about your fear of flying, or any other psychological problem, I suggest shopping around. Selecting a therapist is the same as any other consumer shopping. Prices and quality vary. Talk to your friends and ask if they have any recommendations. Behavioral therapy has the best rate of success when dealing specifically with fear reduction. Regardless of whom or what type of therapist you choose to visit, do ask if he has any experience specifically in treating fear of flying.

Many colleges, service clubs, organizations, airlines, and private counseling firms offer Fear of Flight Clinics. I recommend the majority of these clinics. Some of these clinics are offered free as a community service, and others charge hundreds of dollars for a relatively short course. You can call your local college or travel agency or contact the nearest airline for the names and addresses of classes in your area.

Be Your Own Best Friend

Hopefully, by now you fully understand and agree that being afraid to fly does not mean you are mentally ill or possessed by an evil demon. You also know that confronting your fear is a personal challenge, and that you will need practice to learn to feel comfortable in the face of fear. During your recovery, you will experience all kinds of feelings. Regardless of how you feel, continue on. There really is no other way.

You can function even if panic strikes. Remember, it is always the worst at first. Give yourself a little time and the fear will pass. I know this is a difficult prescription. But it is difficult, not impossible.

Patience and understanding will go a long way in helping you become stronger. I doubt that without some patience and understanding anyone could fully recover. You see, being afraid is a lonely business. Other people cannot see, feel, or relieve your pain. Some friends may feel sorry for you, but the pain is yours and yours alone.

You need to be your own best friend. You have learned that your physical symptoms are nothing but normal, though exaggerated, reactions to stress. You are armed with new knowledge and understanding. You know what you need to do and how to do it.

You are courageous. When you walk off the plane, you are a hero. There will be no crowds of people cheering congratulations. Maybe your wife or husband will give you an "It wasn't so bad, was it?" But only you know how much you accomplished. Be proud of yourself. You deserve it.

10
BEFORE YOU FLY

It would not be very smart to learn about flying and how to practice control over your fears only to drop the ball just when you are about to take off and reach your goal. You have also learned that under stress, thinking becomes impaired. To ensure that you haven't forgotten some of the things you can do to make flying a good experience, I would like you to read this chapter now, again just before your next flight, and possibly even during your next flight.

Preflight Checklist

- Select the least fear-provoking way for you to fly. (If you do not like small planes, take big ones. If you do not like long flights, take shorter ones.)
- Get all tickets, seat selections, and reservations taken care of well in advance. You don't need the extra worry and inconvenience.
- Get plenty of rest.

- Eat before you fly.
- Take aboard the plane whatever will make you feel most comfortable.
- Do not arrange stressful things to do just before or after your flight.
- Don't try to save a few dollars at the cost of not reaching your goal. (Travel first class, buy extra magazines, or go to the airport in a taxi.)
- Remember, if panic does strike—don't add a second fear. It is worst at the first. It will pass and you will be okay.
- Stay as relaxed as possible. If you become tense, use active relaxation.
- If you think you are going to faint, get sick, or run up and down the aisles screaming—you're just scaring yourself. Use thought stoppage.
- Remember, with each success you get stronger.
- Remember your personal goal.
- Be good to yourself.

Sometimes it seems remarkably easy to simply lose sight of why we are doing what we are doing. For example, someone who flies because it is necessary for his business is quite different from a retired couple who plans to take a once-in-a-lifetime trip to South America. One has to master flying, and the other needs only minimal coping skills.

It is also necessary to remind yourself that you have the courage to try. Even though you might not like it, things are the way they are.

We all have our own battles. This is yours—and you can win it.

At times you may feel defective and ashamed. "Why am I like this?" "What is wrong with me?" "Why do I have these problems?" Remember, whatever you think or feel are simply reactions to stress. As painful and scary as it may seem, flying is not dangerous.

In several surveys I conducted, when asked if they ever felt scared or uncomfortable about flying, nearly 80 percent of those surveyed admitted that at times flying bothers them. So you see, you have a lot of company. Due to overly sensitized nerves, your reactions may come on quicker and be more intense than most, but the vast majority of people have some nervous habits or physical reactions that appear in response to flying.

When flying, do not expect to feel completely at ease. For most of us, flying just is not an everyday experience.

Before the Flight

Waiting can be the worst. Before a flight, it is normal to experience some anxiety. If you can survive waiting, you can survive flying. Waiting and worrying cause mental exhaustion and set the scene for a nervous overreaction. It is much like going to the dentist. To sit and wait is usually much worse than the actual event. Even actual pain is often easier than the waiting. Anticipation of pain—this is what fear is all about.

Keeping this is in mind, be sure you do not put yourself under additional stress. Schedule lots of time to get things done. Not too much time though. Getting to the airport four hours before your flight departs is just as silly as arriving at the airport at the very last moment rushed and frazzled. Work not to become overly concerned about the trip. Packing three days before a flight is a sign that you are overpreparing—and probably making a mountain out of a molehill. Exaggeration causes more tension.

I will assume you have done all your scheduling and purchased your tickets in advance. Did you remember to request the seat you wanted? Not sure where to sit? Well, anywhere in the first class section should be nice. If you are traveling coach, try an aisle seat over the wings. The more details you can take care of ahead of time, the less you'll experience stress when it comes time to fly. If parking poses a problem, call a taxi. Do not try to save a few dollars at the cost of your well-being. I have a friend who completely indulges himself when he flies. Fist-class seat, wine aboard the plane, a top-quality hotel, excellent meals, and he uses taxis and porters whenever he can. The way he explains it, "I would rather not fly. When I must, I treat myself like a king. It seems to make the flying worthwhile." I agree. Whatever works.

Even if you don't feel hungry before you fly, eat something. A light meal about two hours before a flight is ideal. I suggest you even take a few goodies with you aboard the airplane. That way if you don't feel like a meal in flight, you can still keep your energy up. This is no time for a strict diet. If you like chocolate chip cookies, then that is exactly what you should have.

A Good Prescription

Anything you can do that helps you keep your mind off the upcoming flight is a good prescription. Don't misunderstand me, I don't want you to avoid your fears. I do want you to avoid dwelling on your fears. I would like you to select at least one thing that you like that you can take with you aboard the plane.

If you enjoy reading, bring a favorite book along. I recall one fearful flier who loved mystery novels. I suggested she select a really good mystery novel and a day before flying read all but the last hundred pages. Our arrangement was that once aboard the plane, she would finish reading the book. If it helps you on the plane, it is probably a good idea.

Again, I am not telling you to avoid your fears. What I am saying is, help yourself.

If reading isn't for you, then maybe it is backgammon, munching on some cookies, crossword puzzles, planning a room addition, playing solitaire, writing letters, playing chess, knitting, doing your nails, listening to music, or drawing. Bring your goodies. Don't just sit and think of your fears. Be active. You will never recover by simply waiting for the flight to end.

Should you start to become uncomfortable, use the active relaxation exercise. Remember, less tension equals less panic. It is physiologically impossible to be relaxed and panic. Relaxation will work—guaranteed.

The Flight

Now for the flight. Upon arriving at the airport, check to ensure that you are not tense. Even if you are frightened, you will be able to function. If you have time, stop in a rest room, freshen up, and take a minute to look at yourself in the mirror. Give yourself a little pep talk.

"Ladies and gentlemen, passengers on Eastern Airlines Flight 692 for Atlanta, Georgia, may now board at Gate 12."

This is it. Relax, there is no hurry. Mosey onto the airplane and find your seat. Maybe a little fresh air (the valve overhead). If you are uncomfortable, use a little active relaxation. Prove again to yourself that you are in control. Say hello to the person nearest you.

From now until you are back on terra firma, these are your goals:

- Be as relaxed as possible (use active relaxation).

- Don't add second fear (use thought stoppage).

- Confront fear (let whatever happens happen; don't resist).

- Enjoy yourself (this is your life, smile).

As the airplane departs, climbs, and flies along, try to remember to avoid becoming preoccupied with yourself. Use the goodies you brought on board to help you from getting caught up in yourself.

Remember, any scary or panicky feelings will vanish.

If you find you are beginning to become tense, go back to the basic active relaxation exercise:

- Take a full breath.
- Count from one to ten while . . .
- Relaxing feet to face.
- Take another deep breath.
- Stretch, bend, and rotate your head.

Normal Anxiety

It is natural to feel some anxiety or excitement before a trip. Predeparture excitement or anxiety is not something to cure. The trick is not to let the excitement get bottled up or get out of hand and grow into an anxiety attack.

Don't resist or run from your experiences. The more you can accept, the more able you will be to effectively and successfully handle your fears.

Flying is safe. In the United States, more than 850,000 people travel by air every day.

Confront, communicate, and continue.

Conclusion

So the wild blue yonder is not so wild after all. Unfortunately, many people still view flying as a dangerous venture rather than as what it is—

the fastest and safest means of transportation in the world.

I guess as long as newspapers flash headlines like SMALL PLANE KILLS FAMILY OF THREE, flying will have an uphill public relations problem.

What I hope you recognize now is that flying is safe and that fear is something produced internally. Fear is a natural emotion, but it sure can get out of hand. If handled improperly, fear can hang around and limit our lives.

In a nutshell, fear of flying is a question of how one perceives flying. If you continue to think of flying as a big deal, it will stay a big deal. The more you can view flying as no big deal, the easier it is going to be for you not to get all worked up.

Maybe someday you will learn to love flying, maybe not. Maybe you will always be a little scared. So what! You can control your fears.

Do not let your fears keep you grounded.

Good luck!